Edinburgh

New Directions for Church in Mission

D1605859

Edinburgh

2010

NEW DIRECTIONS FOR CHURCH IN MISSION

Kenneth R. Ross

WILLIAM CAREY INTERNATIONAL UNIVERSITY PRESS
PASADENA, CALIFORNIA

Edinburgh 2010: New Directions for Church in Mission

Copyright © 2010 by Edinburgh 2010

All rights reserved.

ISBN: 9780865850095
Library of Congress Control Number: 2010923714

Published by William Carey International University Press
1539 E. Howard Street, Pasadena, California 91104

William Carey International University Press publishes works that further the university's objective to prepare men and women to discover and address the roots of human problems around the world.

Printed in the United States of America.

Contents

Preface

One of the most remarkable meetings I have ever attended took place at New College on the Mound in Edinburgh in July 2005. Twenty people, between them broadly representative of world Christianity, met to consider the approach of the centenary of the Edinburgh 1910 World Missionary Conference.

The principal task of the meeting was to identify the topics on which attention should be concentrated in the preparations for the centenary. Inspired by the memory of Edinburgh 1910, when eight Commissions considered the issues thought to be of greatest importance to the missionary movement, the aim was to define the topics which called for attention at the start of the 21st century. Though the group was meeting for the first time and came from a wide diversity of backgrounds, it was able to identify the topics which now form the content of this small book. As many others considered these topics in subsequent years, it was widely acknowledged that these are indeed the crucial matters to be faced in regard to Christian mission today. The themes have energised people around the world to form circles of study and reflection. It is out of these that the content of this book has come.

Most books, to a greater or lesser extent, owe their origins to the interaction among a group of people. It is therefore common in a Preface for the author to acknowledge their debt to all who contributed to the book's development. In the case of this little book, the debt is much greater than normal. What it offers is a reading of the fruits of the Edinburgh 2010 study process and it is therefore almost entirely dependent on the work which has been done by the hundreds of people all over the world who have been involved in it, in one way or another, and particularly by the Conveners of the nine study tracks.

It owes a more immediate debt to the edited version of the results of the study process—Edinburgh 2010: Witnessing to Christ Today, edited by Daryl Balia and Kirsteen Kim and published by Regnum in Oxford in 2010. To a great extent, this small book is a condensed version of that larger volume. It is a reading or interpretation of material which can be found in the larger book in greater depth and detail. I am grateful to members of the Edinburgh 2010 Study Process Monitoring Group, particularly Daryl Balia, Knud Jorgensen and Kirsteen Kim for their critical feedback on the text. I was also greatly helped by Robert Calvert, Tony Foreman and Shirley Fraser who each offered comments and suggestions which significantly strengthened the analysis.

My aim has been to distil the essence of the material yielded by the Edinburgh 2010 study process. I have attempted to use non-technical language and to state the issues succinctly so that they may be readily accessible to the ordinary church member or enquirer. For the shortcomings in interpretation I accept full responsibility. Others may interpret differently or have different emphases. Nonetheless, I very much hope that my distillation will provide a good starting place for those wishing to engage the rich material created through the Edinburgh 2010 process.

All Bible references are from the English Standard Version (London: Collins, 2002) and I am grateful to the publisher for permission to include biblical quotations.

Kenneth R. Ross
Edinburgh, February 2010

Introduction

The centenary of the "Edinburgh 1910" World Missionary Conference has proved to be a suggestive moment for those concerned with the question of how the church of Jesus Christ engages the world in which it is set. "Edinburgh 2010" has succeeded in bringing together a broader representation of world Christianity than has ever before been mobilised in a common project. As will be apparent on the pages which follow, it has been able to draw on the experience and insights of people from every continent. It has also been enriched by the gifts and wisdom of almost every conceivable Christian tradition—from Eastern Orthodox and Roman Catholic to Pentecostal and Independent. Its various meetings and consultations have included women and men, young and old, fresh and experienced. Inasmuch the delegates to Edinburgh 1910 were predominantly white, Western, Protestant, male and elderly, Edinburgh 2010 has accepted the challenge to ensure that voices unheard a century ago are prominent today. The process is therefore informed by possibly a wider range of experience than has ever before been applied to questions of church and mission. For further background on Edinburgh 1910 and Edinburgh 2010 the reader is referred to the companion volume *Edinburgh 2010: Springboard for Mission.*[1]

At the heart of the process leading to Edinburgh 2010 have been nine study groups, each tasked to consider one of the crucial questions facing Christian mission today. It is their work which underlies the nine chapters of this book. Each chapter is an attempt to reflect the findings of a study group in a short and straightforward way designed to provoke further discussion. Each is equally valuable and the book might best be imagined as a circle of chapters with each shedding its own particular light on the question of mission. There is therefore no requirement to begin at the beginning and finish at the end. The reader should feel free to select topics of particular interest and begin with these. At the same time, it is hoped that a natural flow will be apparent to those who choose to read consecutively from beginning to end. The book makes no attempt to cover all that needs to be said about church or mission. Indeed there are matters of great moment which it is not able to discuss in any depth or detail. Its focus is firmly on the points at which there may be new directions for the church, in mission, to take at this time.

Each study group had a clearly defined topic which provided its starting point. Study of the topic led to points of connection with other study tracks. It will therefore be apparent in this text that there are points of convergence and overlap between the different chapters. These, perhaps, are the points which particularly call for our attention. Each chapter concludes with a biblical text to ponder, some questions to consider and a prayer to offer. These resources can be used individually but may be particularly useful in the context of a study group.

For purposes of shorthand it has become customary to delineate the world by points of the compass—Western, non-Western, Near East, Far East and so on. Recently a convention has developed to describe Europe and North America as the "North" while Latin America, Africa, Asia and Oceania are described as the "Global South". Inevitably it is an imprecise division—Australia and New Zealand, for example, are in the southern hemisphere but are not regarded as part of the "Global South" in economic and cultural terms. It is, however, a distinction which is particularly pertinent to consideration of Christian mission at this time. In the interests of consistency throughout the book, the terminology of "North" and "Global South" has been used to differentiate what in 1910 were described respectively as "the Christian world" and "the mission field".

Edinburgh 2010 has a focus on a particular date and place. The first week of June 2010 will see a highly international assembly of some 250 people meeting in Edinburgh to recognise the centenary of the 1910 World Missionary Conference, to absorb the results of the centennial study process and to attempt to discern the way forward for Christian mission worldwide. In view of good economy and environmental responsibility, the number gathered in Edinburgh will be relatively small. The aim of the project, however, is that many more will participate through the web site and through events in their own localities. The purpose of this small book is to provide an accessible introduction to the material which will inform the Edinburgh 2010 conference. For all who wish to connect with this agenda, it offers a place to start, whether before the conference or afterwards. It aims to be a valuable resource for all who are engaged in exploring what Christian mission will mean in the world of the 21st century. To navigate today's world for purposes of mission is an exercise that cannot be completed by depending on old maps. The careful and newly completed mapping found in these pages provides a basis for the church in mission to find new directions.

1

Local Church—Your Time Has Come

MISSION TODAY—LOCAL CHURCH TAKES THE LEAD

In the great missionary movement which transformed world Christianity in the 19th and 20th centuries, mission was regarded as a matter for the professionals. Missionary societies, church mission boards and missionary orders were formed to take responsibility for this dimension of Christian witness. Local churches were encouraged to be supportive—by prayer, by financial giving and by providing recruits to the missionary movement. They were not expected to be missionary bodies themselves.

At the beginning of the 21st century, a new pattern began to emerge. As the church has put down roots in almost every part of the world the question is how well are churches equipped to fulfil the missionary mandate? No longer are church and mission viewed as two separate matters. Now the focus is on their integral relation to one another: "the church of the mission" and "the mission of the church".

Viewed in this light, the local church now takes centre stage as the primary instrument of mission. Everywhere that God's people gather for worship, fellowship and witness, they are the footprint of the universal church. The local church is not merely a branch of an organisation which has its HQ elsewhere. Rather, it is at the local level that the universal church finds its authentic life and expression. Local churches therefore hold the initiative, not least when it comes to the mission dimension which is essential to the life of any true church.

As local churches grasp this responsibility, many are experimenting with different models. The inherited parish structure with a priest/pastor "in charge" of each parish may not be the best model for today. In some parts of the world house churches are a fast-growing movement. These have no church building, no professional leadership and are sometimes considered subversive. In other contexts "emerging" churches experiment with less structured forms of church life. Seeking to transform secular space, they gather in cafes, dance clubs or on riverbanks, fostering a spirituality that is integrated into everyday life. Some are so alienated from institutional church life that they live their Christian life without a regular church, perhaps connecting with one or more movements of spiritual renewal. Others continue to value traditional buildings and a more structured form of worship but undergo a more subtle transformation as they adjust to our contemporary situation.

Common to all these approaches to the development of local church life is a rediscovery of "the priesthood of all believers". Gone are the days when leadership and responsibility in church life were the exclusive preserve of the clergy. Increasingly, churches are developing a pattern of life where all members encourage one another to discover their gifts and exercise their ministry. The role of the professional pastor is then to foster and strengthen the ministry of all the believers.

One outcome of this emerging pattern of ministry is that churches become more "missional" in their life and witness.

Rather than mission being something that is remitted to dedicated professionals, it is seen to be the responsibility of all. Expectations and structures are developed which enable the local church to reach out in Christ's name—both close to home and far away. Imagination is kindled to consider how to communicate the gospel in our own culture as well as in other cultures elsewhere in the world. The "go-structures" which once were the preserve of specialist missionary societies are now being built into the life of the local church.

Vulnerability and Mission

Mwizero is an elderly Batwa woman from Burundi in eastern Africa. She lives with a group of widows in a makeshift grass hut. She has no food, no home and cannot read or write. She has no country; she is a pygmy and her neighbours do not consider her a human being. If she falls sick she cannot visit a hospital nor can she register a marriage. If someone would kill her, it would not be murder; she is, after all, not a human being. She has no church though she knows and believes that there is a God who will remember her.

Nirma Rani, a Dalit girl student from India was slapped for saying *Namaste* to a Brahmin teacher and her father was beaten up later for questioning such an act. Caste is practised in schools where Dalit children occupy separate seats given to them. Dhanam lost her eye when she was beaten up by her teacher for helping herself to drinking water from a pot without waiting to be served by a caste person. She had polluted the water by her touch.

Christian mission is biased to the poor. It is mindful that, in the story of Jesus, God becomes vulnerable and identifies with the poor and marginalised. It is aware, moreover, that God undertakes a mission of transformation from that position of weakness. This is the meaning of the cross.

Today most church members worldwide are found not among the wealthy and powerful but rather among the poor and vulnerable. What does it mean for mission when its agents come mainly from contexts of poverty and exclusion?

Over the years many missionaries have chosen to make themselves vulnerable. They have exposed themselves to a new and unfamiliar situation. They have accepted insecurity and material poverty. They have embarked on the task of learning a new language, invariably going through a time of weakness and frustration. However, many church members have not chosen vulnerability. Rather, they have been born into it and have lived with it all their days.

Those accustomed to living with vulnerability have little to lose and are often ready to take risks and be open to others in a way which would not come easily to those who are used to power and privilege. They also have a motivation, which could easily elude their more comfortable fellow Christians, to work with God for transformation. They are sensitive to the death-dealing forces, structures and systems which threaten human flourishing. Their prayer for the kingdom of God to come has a depth and potency which is rarely found among the prosperous. The poor therefore have a leading role in the mission of God in the world today. The task of the rest of the church is to identify with the poor as they participate in the vulnerable mission of God.

> There is an element of mystery when the dynamism of mission does not come from the people of a position of power or privilege ... but from below, from the little ones, those who have few material, financial or technical resources.[2]

—Samuel Escobar, Peru

CHILDREN AND MISSION

Recent years have seen an awakening to the role of children and young people in Christian mission. In one sense, this is nothing new since for many years mission agencies have offered care and education to children. What is new is a heightened awareness of the significance of children in the Bible and in the mission of God. We live at a time when many countries have a predominantly young population. There is greater understanding of the receptivity of children and youth, and of their potential as a force for mission and transformation.

Biblical stories, such as those of Samuel or David or Jesus, show how God uses children to fulfil his purposes. In the Bible, children are not regarded only as those who might in future play a role in the kingdom of God. They are already engaged as children, in crucial ways, in the unfolding purpose of God. Jesus hints that children may have more capacity than adults to relate to God and be agents of God's mission.

> Patricia is a twelve-year-old girl living in the slum community of Santa Mesa in the Philippines. This community is known as a breeding ground for thieves, criminals, and sex workers. Patricia saw how the children of her neighbourhood were dishevelled, and deprived, so she started teaching five- to ten-year-olds the Bible. She gathers them together once a week, tells them about Jesus, and says she doesn't want them to grow up to be criminals, but to know about Jesus.

> Terrorist bombings, beheadings, and raids on villages by Islamic jihadists have plagued the people of central Sulawesi, Indonesia in recent years. After winning a preaching contest last December, eight-year-old Moko travelled to nearby towns to preach God's word to the people. While the people worship, Moko's friend Selfin prays for a touch from God. Aside from physical healing, Moko also preaches about the healing of his homeland, and his hometown of Poso. In his sermons Moko

speaks of peace, reconciliation and forgiveness based on Jesus' command that people should love one another.

Pronchai is a fifteen-year-old boy from an isolated minority tribal group in Thailand. For schooling, he moved to the city, where drugs are far too familiar to children and around which bad environmental practices are used, such as forest-burning. Pronchai has shown himself to be a leader, and became the initiator of several community activities, such as environmental care and drug prevention Initiatives. As a result, his school received the "clean school without drugs" award from the Princess of Thailand.

The vast majority of those who choose to follow Jesus take their decision between the ages of 4 and 14. Of these, a large majority indicate that they were drawn to faith in Jesus Christ by the witness of their peers. Most often, it is children who lead their age-mates to an experience of faith. Children therefore have a strategic role to play in the mission of God. Rather than being left on the sidelines, their place must be at the heart of the missionary life of the church. A priority for the church is to equip its children for ministry and mission and then to ensure that they have full opportunity to exercise their gifts.

MISSION IN THE AGE OF THE NETWORK

Edinburgh 1910 was energised by a shared desire to develop greater collaboration and cooperation among those engaged in Christian mission. It marked the birth of the ecumenical movement. The 20th century has seen great strides forward in terms of greater understanding and shared action among Christians of different stripes. It also saw new fault lines emerging and a resultant sense of fragmentation.

There remains a powerful mandate for collaborative working. It is rooted in:

- God's Trinitarian being;

- the prayer of Jesus that "they all may be one";

- the strategic advantages of working together.

In the 21st century a new opportunity to fulfil this mandate emerges as we enter the age of the network.

It has been suggested that *hierarchy* was the model of social interaction in an agrarian culture and that bureaucracy was the appropriate model for the industrial culture which emerged in the 19th and 20th centuries. For the information culture which emerged from the late 20th century, the *network* is the required model. The decisive question is not what is your place in the hierarchy nor whether your skill set fits the purpose of the bureaucracy. Everything hinges on the question of what links you have, how connected you are. The network model seems to resonate with the New Testament—its images of the body or the vine and its interconnected apostolic initiatives. The whole movement which has made people disciples of Christ across the centuries can readily be understood as a network.

As models inherited from the bureaucratic age falter, Christians find new energy and new possibilities in fast-moving networks. These are often informal in nature and can easily cut across boundaries once thought to be impregnable. They have the capacity to fire imagination and to empower people to make common cause. This enables them to mobilise resources quickly to meet strategic mission objectives.

On a global scale, a special challenge today lies in the interaction of "North" and "South". The Northern world has been used to having the initiative, still has the lion's share of the material resources but suffers from a crisis of confidence. The Global South is energised by revival movements but, in the day of its strength, is vulnerable to the craving for power. To create partnerships through which the complementary strengths of North and South can be mobilised in the mission of God—this is one of the greatest challenges facing the churches today.

It is a challenge brought home to many by the impact of the movement through which Christians from the Global South migrate to Northern countries which they now regard as a crucial mission field. Diaspora networks bring vibrant Christian faith into the countries of the North from which they first received the gospel but which are now highly secularised. For Northerners it is a new experience to be on the receiving end of mission. For migrants from the Global South there is the new challenge of crossing the cultural boundary which separates them from the heart and mind of the secular North. In the melting pot of urban life today, effective partnership between North and South holds the potential for an almost unlimited range of cross-cultural mission initiatives.

The dynamics of Christian mission today have:
- placed the local church at centre stage;
- demonstrated that it is through vulnerability that God's saving work is done;
- highlighted the crucial role of children in the mission of God;
- shown the power of networks and partnerships for mission.

Can we hear the call of God to initiative, vulnerability, inclusion and networking?

Key Text: Ephesians 4:7, 11-16

But grace was given to each one of us according to the measure of Christ's gift .... And he gave the apostles, the prophets, the evangelists, the shepherds and teachers, to equip the saints for the work of ministry, for building up the body of Christ, until we all attain to the unity of the faith and of the knowledge of the Son of God, to mature manhood, to the measure of the stature of the fullness of Christ, so that we may no longer be children, tossed to and fro with the waves and carried about by every wind of doctrine, by human cunning, by craftiness in deceitful schemes. Rather, speaking the truth in love, we are to grow up in every way into him who is the head, into Christ, from whom the whole body, joined and held together by every joint with which it is equipped, when each part is working properly, makes the body grow so that it builds itself up in love.

QUESTIONS FOR DISCUSSION

Why has the present time been identified as a moment when there is unprecedented opportunity to fulfil the vision set out in this text?

What are the implications of the shift from mission societies to local churches as the driving force of the church's missionary dimension?

Who or what do you think will be the primary agents of Christian mission in the 21st century?

PRAYER

I praise you, O God, for your mission in Jesus Christ, unfolding from age to age in ever new shapes and forms.
Help me not to be stuck in the old ways, however cherished,
but to be in step with the new things you are doing today.
I marvel, O Lord, that your strength is made known through weakness,
and that there is always a surprise factor in the agents you choose to do your work.

Grant me the vision to see the lines along which your mission runs today,
and the courage to play my part in breaking new ground.
All for your glory, through Jesus Christ your Son. Amen

2

What Is Mission?

MISSION: ESSENTIAL OR EMBARRASSING?

Essential to Christianity is its missionary character. It is a faith with outreach built into it. Anyone who reads the Gospel of Matthew will not finish without being addressed by the command of Jesus: "Go therefore and make disciples of all nations" (Matthew 28:19). Read the Gospel of Mark and you encounter Jesus saying in conclusion: "Go into all the world and proclaim the gospel to the whole creation" (Mark 16:15).

Anyone who is a member of the church has, at one time or another, been on the receiving end of such proclamation. Someone has told them the good news of Jesus Christ in such a way that they have decided it is worthwhile to belong to the church, the community of those who believe in Jesus Christ as Saviour. Soon they realise that the church has a job to do in the world. It is not intended to be preoccupied with its own internal life. Its members, following Jesus, are expected to minister to others, whether nearby or far away. Mission is in the DNA of the church.

Yet mission, for many church members, has become a source of embarrassment, misunderstanding and confusion. It conjures

19

up images of missionaries in pith helmets who apparently colluded with long-discredited imperialism and colonialism. It smacks of coercion and lack of sensitivity to the culture and faith of others. It suggests a crude and excessive religious zeal. Is the idea of "mission" carrying so much unwelcome baggage that it would be better to be discarded?

When you are aware, on the one hand, that mission is essential to Christian faith and, on the other hand, that it has become a problematic idea, it is time to ask *what is truly the meaning of mission?* This was not a question on which the delegates to the great Edinburgh 1910 World Missionary Conference felt that they had to spend a lot of time. They were united by the conviction that their task was to take the gospel *from* "the Christian world" where it was well known *to* the "non-Christian world" where it was little known. The discussion was concerned with the means and the methods. A century later, we have to take up the discussion at the more fundamental level of determining the meaning of mission.

MISSION: LEARNING FROM EXPERIENCE

One thing we have learned in the course of the century is that our understanding is conditioned by our vantage point. More than they realised, the Edinburgh 1910 delegates looked at the world from the vantage point of Westerners at a time when the Western powers dominated world affairs and colonial rule was at its height. Their missionary purpose could very easily be conflated with the spread of Western culture and values. Mission was understood very differently by those who were on the receiving-end of Western-based missionary work. They were active in interpreting it in their own way and using it for their own purposes. Today our understanding of mission must be informed by all who are practically involved, not only those who occupy positions of power.

The Edinburgh 2010 study process included a focus on a Dalit community in Vegeswarapuram, a village in West Godavari district of Andhra Pradesh, south India. Dalits are "outcaste" communities previously known as "untouchables". Their first experience of Christian mission came in their interaction with foreign missionaries who settled in their area and established networks of schools, hospitals, hostels and churches. Here Dalits both received the gospel of Jesus Christ, forming active church communities and created a base from which they could assert their identity and take their rightful place in the wider society. From their point of view, the colonizing forces were found amongst the powerful within their own society. Mission empowered them in their quest for liberation from oppression. The self-respect which they discovered through their faith and Christian discipleship strengthened them for the struggle for social justice which extended far beyond the boundaries of church life. For them mission comprises both the proclamation of the gospel which builds up the life of the church and the struggle for social justice and against casteism which unites them with a broad coalition united by this common purpose.[3]

Current experience worldwide teaches us that mission has different dimensions and can be understood in different ways. (1) Those who study mission have laid emphasis on the idea of the mission of God (*missio Dei*)—a comprehensive understanding of all that God is doing in human life and history. (2) Those who are responsible for the mission practice of the churches have laid emphasis on mission as proclamation—making known the good news about Jesus Christ. (3) Those who are coming from a position of disadvantage or oppression have laid emphasis on mission as the struggle for justice and liberation. Some, like the Dalit community mentioned above, have achieved a measure of integration of different understandings of mission. For others, the different dimensions of mission are held in unresolved tension.

In fact, it is not a matter of mutually exclusive models where we have to choose one or another. Rather, differing models overlap and interconnect. A balanced understanding of mission will be informed by a wide range of experience and will reflect more than one emphasis. Rather than championing one view to the exclusion of others, we can learn from experience that there are a rich variety of ways to witness to Jesus Christ in each context. We have much to learn from those who bring perspectives that contrast with our own. So long as the witness being offered is one which points us to Jesus Christ crucified and risen, it is one from which our own understanding can be extended and enriched.

MISSION: EXPRESSION OF THE LIFE OF GOD

The past century's reflection on the meaning of mission has shown that we need to push beyond thinking of mission in terms of human activity to find its deepest foundations within the life of God. At the heart of the Christian confession is the Trinitarian nature of God: the Father, the Son and the Holy Spirit. This, however, has often been regarded as an advanced and difficult topic, only to be considered after more accessible aspects of the faith have been clarified. Recent reflection has suggested, on the other hand, that this is the point at which to begin in order to develop a proper understanding of Christian mission. It is within the dynamic relationships found in the life of God that *sending* first takes place. The Father sends the Son. The Son sends the Spirit. Here is where mission begins and finds its essential meaning. We are not required to invent a mission of our own. It is ours to join in with the mission of God.

This leads us to a fresh appreciation of the role of the Holy Spirit as the agent of mission. The worldwide Pentecostal movement has emphasised the power of the Spirit and has awakened all Christians to this dimension. In the earlier history of the church, the West understood the Holy Spirit as the agent of Christ to fulfil the task of mission while the East emphasised the Holy Spirit as the source of Christ and the church, gathering the people of God in his kingdom and then going forth in mission.

Today Christians with a background in primal religion are alert to the reality of the realm of the spirits and are therefore open to the ministry of the Holy Spirit in a particularly powerful way. This has helped to put a renewed focus on the role of the Holy Spirit in the life and ministry of Jesus as a key to understanding the way in which the Spirit works in the world today. The intimate connection of Christ and the Spirit allows us to develop a broad understanding of God's action in the world, yet one which has Christ at its centre.

The church is challenged and enabled by the Spirit to truly reflect Jesus Christ in the way it engages with the world around it. The Spirit empowers the church to engage effectively with such matters as justice in the local community and care for the entire created order. The Spirit ever brings the reminder that Christ is not contained within the church but rather is discovered and experienced as the church meets the challenges of mission. The proclamation which makes Christ known in the context of worship needs to be complemented by the power of the Spirit demonstrated in loving relationships and committed action for justice and reconciliation.

The meaning of mission is found not only with reference to the life of the church but equally to the kingdom of God—of which Jesus so often spoke. The new social, spiritual and cosmic reality which Jesus has inaugurated provides a broad context for consideration of mission. This is not to undermine the proclamation of the good news of Jesus Christ nor the life of the church which is formed in response to that proclamation. However, it does demonstrate that to be called into the life of the church is also to participate in the coming of Christ's kingdom. This means that our personal experience of faith is stretched to embrace concerns for justice in the community, peace in the world and the integrity of the creation. None of these can be excluded when our concern is with the coming of the kingdom of God in time and space. It leads us, for example, to combat unjust and destructive economic models and to promote "the economy of the enough". It prompts us to resist threats to the integrity of creation like global warming or nuclear weapons.

MODELS OF MISSION FOR THE 21ST CENTURY
Mission will be defined in the years to come not by any single master model but by looking through the lenses provided by a variety of models. Among them are liberation, dialogue, and reconciliation.

Mission as liberation
Where Christians have drawn on their faith to expose and overcome unjust political and social structures they have defined mission in terms of liberation. This model draws attention to Jesus' identification with the poor and his confrontation with the forces of "mammon". It notes the challenge which Jesus brought to ruling religious elites and colonial powers—a clash which ultimately led to Jesus being put to death. Reading the gospel story in this way fosters a critical approach to our contemporary society. Forces of oppression and impoverishment are exposed. Jesus is seen as the one who brings freedom. The gospel imperative is to act in ways which bring life to others, especially the poor and marginalised. There remains a transcendent dimension to salvation but the practical focus is on action which makes for justice and freedom in today's world.

Mission as dialogue

As many societies have experienced increasing plurality in the religious adherence of citizens, there has been a growth of inter-faith dialogue. This has sometimes been perceived as a threat to mission—and vice versa. Yet in societies with long experience of religious plurality, particularly in Asia, Christians have found ways of engaging in respectful dialogue with neighbours who profess another faith while at the same time developing projects of mission and service which demonstrate the love of God. In a global context where there is an imperative for mutual respect between religious communities, dialogue may be the most appropriate way in which to witness to neighbours. A broad view of the work of the Holy Spirit in creation, in contemporary movements, in spiritualities and in individuals allows for a positive approach to dialogue. It is expected that evidence of the presence and activity of the Spirit will be discerned in the experience and perspectives of dialogue partners. Where this is found to be true to Jesus Christ, Christians can have confidence that the Spirit is at work. In a world of many faiths and worldviews, dialogue may often be the most appropriate way for mission to take effect.

Mission as reconciliation

As the 21st century began with a world full of conflict and fractured relationships, attention turned to a major dimension of the New Testament witness: reconciliation and healing. Reconciliation is needed at many levels: between humanity and God; between humans as individuals, communities and cultures; and between humans and the whole of creation. This gives strong resonance to the biblical promise of all things being reconciled in Jesus Christ. The healing ministry of Jesus is given renewed attention in this context—the power of the gospel to transform situations of disease and distress. Thinking of mission in terms of reconciliation and healing draws together a wide range of dimensions—from personal conversion grounded in Christ's sacrificial atonement to the peacemaking activity which reflects the same commitment at the level of inter-communal conflict or international relations.

UNDERSTANDING MISSION TODAY

There is no simple formula which will allow us to comprehend all that is involved in the mission of Christ. We need more than one concept to grasp it all. Edinburgh 1910's passionate desire to take the good news of Jesus to places where it is unknown remains at the heart of mission. Likewise, the planting and nurturing of the church continues to be a core concern. At the same time, our understanding needs to be broadened and deepened if we are to benefit from the past 100 years of experience and be equipped for mission in the complex and interconnected world of the 21st century.

KEY TEXT: JOHN 20:19-23

On the evening of that day, the first day of the week, the doors being locked where the disciples were for fear of the Jews, Jesus came and stood among them and said to them, "Peace be with you." When he had said this, he showed them his hands and his side. Then the disciples were glad when they saw the Lord. Jesus said to them again, "Peace be with you. As the Father sent me, even so am I sending you." And when he had said this, he breathed on them and said to them, "Receive the Holy Spirit. If you forgive the sins of any, they are forgiven them; if you withhold forgiveness from any, it is withheld."

QUESTIONS FOR DISCUSSION

What images come to your mind when you hear the term "mission"?

What does the Father's sending of Jesus mean for Jesus' sending of us?

What does it mean for us that the Holy Spirit is given to us when we are sent forth in mission?

PRAYER

I praise you, O Lord, that you are the God of mission,
that you reach out in love
to bring redemption to the world you have made.
Thank you that Jesus Christ is good news for all people everywhere.
Grant, I pray, that your Holy Spirit would empower me for mission.
Give me a big picture of what you are doing in the world.
Give me the courage to stretch my understanding, to open my heart,
and to step out in faith to live the good news where it is needed most.
For the sake of Jesus Christ the risen Lord. Amen

3

What Motivates Mission?

THE SPIRITUALITY OF MISSION

We often think of mission in terms of its outward engagement. This chapter turns the focus inward and asks what is the motivation for mission. What are the inner springs from which it arises? How does inward experience of the Holy Spirit relate to the outward action of mission? These questions are pursued by tuning in to the experience of a number of constituencies which were not represented at Edinburgh 1910 but which make a very significant contribution to worldwide Christian mission today.

AFRICAN INDEPENDENT CHURCHES

For millions of Africans the crisis they have faced at political, cultural and religious levels is most satisfactorily addressed by African Independent Churches (AICs). These Churches are not affiliated to any parent body outside Africa and express their faith in ways which are attuned to the African cultural context. By and large, they have understood themselves as being engaged in mission from the margins. They are not aligned with any centre of power. Drawing on the African tradition, the AICs are strongly oriented to the community. They resist any separation of the spiritual and the physical. They believe that the Holy Spirit is active in relation to such urgent community issues as HIV/AIDS, unemployment and homelessness. Their spirituality is proactive and holistic.

The mission engagement of the AICs is sustained by prayer, the inspiration of the Holy Spirit and the reading of the Bible. Their location on the margins of societies gives them a spiritual sensitivity which sustains them in face of adversity. Is this a point at which they give a lead to the rest of the church? Though sometimes limited by a tendency to separatism and a lack of theological maturity, their dependence on the Holy Spirit in a context of marginality and lack of resources is something from which the rest of the church has much to learn.

CHINA: THE BACK TO JERUSALEM MOVEMENT

Prior to the Communist Revolution in China, some church leaders conceived a vision of the Chinese church initiating a westward missionary movement that would take the gospel through central Asia to the lands of the Middle East. The dream was that this missionary movement would represent a final leg of world evangelisation, taking the gospel "back to Jerusalem". In this way China would have a special role to play in fulfilling Christ's mandate to "make disciples of all nations".

In the early years of the 21st century, with Christianity growing in China at an unprecedented rate, the vision has been revived. The earlier movement reached as far as Kashgar in western China where it successfully planted churches which are flourishing today. Otherwise it stalled and the dream remained unfulfilled. Today the revived movement has seen Chinese

Christians, inspired by missionary vision, moving to Middle Eastern countries like Iraq. There can be no question that the Back to Jerusalem movement reflects the dynamism of Christianity in China today. However, significant weaknesses are evident. So far, those involved have not learned the Arabic language, limiting their effectiveness in the Middle Eastern context. One group demonstrated great missionary zeal but found that, as itinerant pig herders, it was very difficult for them to find acceptance in Islamic societies. There is a general trend of outward migration from China, driven by economic factors. It has therefore been suggested that there may be mixed motives among some of those participating in the Back to Jerusalem movement.

Similar criticisms were levelled, sometimes deservedly, at European and North American missionaries in the 19th and 20th centuries. So perhaps it should be no surprise to find such issues as mixed motives and lack of cultural sensitivity presenting themselves in the early stages of a new missionary movement. The greatest significance of the Back to Jerusalem movement may be that it illustrates the extent to which today's missionary movement operates "from everywhere to everywhere". The boldness of the vision and the zeal with which it is implemented demonstrate the imagination and vitality of mission in the Global South.

CHURCH MISSION SOCIETY—AFRICA

The Church Missionary Society began more than 200 years ago in England. In 2009 the African part of CMS became autonomous and took the opportunity to cast a vision of mission in Africa. They celebrate the massive church growth which has taken place in Africa but identify a lack of discipleship as the key issue to be addressed.

In particular, their analysis reveals that the process of Christian conversion has failed to address very significant elements in African life and experience. As a result, many experience a "schizophrenia" between their African and their Christian identity. There is an urgent need for an integrated experience and lifestyle if the African church is to have a healthy mission spirituality. The philosophy is to retain the best of the African worldview that is not at odds with the gospel and to challenge that which is.

> The African indigenous church movement largely grew out of this failure by the church to address pertinent issues rooted in the African culture and religion. African cultural practices such as polygamy, witch doctoring, the place of ancestral spirits, clan and communal responsibility left African Christians hanging and the result has been Christians torn between the two worlds.[4]

—Serah Wambua

The spirituality being sought is one which will engage social, political, business and environmental concerns rather than being restricted to personal piety. Business as Mission is one initiative which seeks to have wide-ranging impact. Working from a faith basis this movement seeks to engage the challenge of poverty in Africa by empowering and inspiring business people in Africa to create jobs and make wealth. Countering Afro-pessimism, it seeks to capitalise on Africa's extraordinary strength in terms of people and natural resources.

A KOREAN IMMIGRANT CHURCH

Grace Korean Church in southern California is a church which has come into being through the immigration of Koreans to the USA. Its founder Kwang-shin Kim fostered a strong mission ethos. The goal of mission is proclamation of the gospel and the establishment of strong local congregations in challenging places. This is grounded in a very strong commitment to prayer and finds expression in a wide range of community development programmes in places where the church is active in mission.

The missionary purpose of the church is very prominent. Banners in the church lobby display such slogans as "mission is prayer", "mission is war" or "mission is martyrdom". Those who offer for missionary service are treated as heroes. It is made clear that the primary purpose of the church is to support them. Moreover, all church members are expected to be active in mission. For example, jumbo jets were chartered to fly hundreds of church members on mission trips to Russia at the special time of opportunity identified at the end of the Cold War.

The regular worship of the church places strong emphasis on missionary outreach. The preaching often includes passionate appeals to members to offer themselves for missionary service. Prayer is often focussed on missionaries and the development of their work. Sacrificial financial giving is strongly promoted. The church ensures that at least 50% of its gross income is dedicated to missionary work. Additionally, many members contribute generously to help meet particular needs. Church members are expected to personally visit a mission field, at their own expense, at least once each year.

THE RUSSIAN ORTHODOX CHURCH

Historically, mission has been understood in the Russian Orthodox Church as a matter of forming and strengthening God's people. This has recently changed in response to the long period of Communist rule and the need to reach generations which grew up outside the influence of the church. In 1995, for the first time a Mission Department was established to pioneer and coordinate the work of reaching out to those unfamiliar with the church and the gospel. Strongly centred on the church and its sacramental life, an understanding of mission emerged which also stressed a re-evangelisation of large areas of Russia which lost their historic faith under the impact of atheistic Communist rule.

> The Orthodox mission aims at teaching the peoples to be enlightened in the truths of the faith, at educating people to enable them to live a Christ-like life, and mainly at passing on the experience of communion with God through a personal participation of the believers in the sacramental life of the Eucharistic community.[5]

—Valentin Kozhuharov

The internal strengthening of the church remains very closely integrated with the task of reaching out to unbelievers. For example, when railway trains are used to develop outreach in Siberia, more than 15,000km from Moscow, a special carriage is equipped as a church sanctuary. Thousands of people in the vast territory of eastern Russia have been drawn into the Orthodox faith through such outreach. A healthy worshipping life centred around the eucharist (holy communion) is understood to be the most effective form of outreach.

KOREAN MEGA-CHURCHES

The largest church in the world is Yoido Full Gospel Church in Seoul, South Korea. It has 750,000 members attending on a regular basis. Founded by David Yongi Cho, it represents a contextualised form of classical Pentecostalism. It places strong emphasis on evangelism, both at home and overseas. It has been responsible for the planting of some 500 congregations within Korea, some quite large. It supports extensive missionary work in many countries around the world. It also undertakes social services and engages contemporary social issues, particularly through its *Kukmin Daily Newspaper*.

The life of Yoido Full Gospel Church is rooted in the experience of encounter with God. This is exemplified in the "deathbed" conversion of David Yongi Cho when he was healed from a severe case of tuberculosis. It is also based on an experience of suffering, since the church was formed in the aftermath of the Korean War which inflicted great privation and anguish. Many of the early members of the church came from a background of dispossession, dislocation and many painful experiences. The empowerment of the Holy Spirit is a key emphasis of the ministry, with members often being urged to undergo the "baptism of the Holy Spirit".

Worship forms the base from which to engage in mission. Examples of mission engagement figure prominently in worship services, often through video footage. There is a pronounced emphasis on prayer. Every day an overnight prayer meeting is held, as well as numerous dawn prayer meetings. The church's international prayer mountain is crowded with people who are praying and fasting for up to 40 days. Sacrificial giving, particularly for the support of missions, is strongly encouraged.

Youngnak Presbyterian Church is another very large congregation in Seoul which has a similar high level of commitment to mission, both at home and overseas. One of its distinguishing features is its dedication to the Korean nation. It is linked with patriotism since its origins go back to the Japanese occupation and the Communist takeover, both of which regarded Christianity as an ideological enemy. The reunification of the Korean peninsula is prominent in the prayers of the church. It has undertaken evangelism on a large scale, establishing more than 600 churches in South Korea. Outreach within the army is a particular emphasis. It has a particular focus on education and runs an extensive range of social service, relief and development projects spread across many countries.

INDIAN MISSION SPIRITUALITY

Sadhu Singh and Narayana Tilak, early—20th—century church leaders, still provide inspiration for the development of Indian mission spirituality. They refused to be confined to institutions or to particular sectors of society. Rather they embraced the rich Indian spiritual tradition and commended Jesus by the quality of their faith and devotion. Their emphasis on direct experience of Jesus enabled Christianity to break out of its foreign appearance and take on a genuinely Indian character. The accounts of their life-changing encounters with Jesus were ones to which Indians could readily relate.

For Christian faith to take root in Indian soil and be accessible to the majority, it needs to look beyond sustaining institutions and engaging in polemical debates. In the Indian context it can best be commended by sincere lives of true devotion to Jesus as a path of discipleship. An authentic, sacrificial and reflective faith will be considered on its own terms among the peoples of India, inviting them into an experience with its own attractive power.

Mission Spirituality for the 21st Century

For mission to retain its authentic character it has to be nourished by its spirituality. A note being struck today is the importance of recognising that God is already at work in the contexts to which the church brings the gospel. Identifying the ways in which God is working and how these prepare the way for the gospel is a matter of discernment requiring mature spirituality. Given the historical baggage which comes with the term "mission", might it be better to speak of a path of discipleship which all are invited to walk. The holistic character of Christian mission is widely emphasised, as the church worldwide breaks free of the European Enlightenment with its tendency to compartmentalise. Openness, transparency and inclusiveness are also much desired in a divided and mistrustful world. Those concerned with the mission agenda dare not neglect the cultivation of the required spirituality.

Christian spirituality is a gift and a task. It requires communion with God (contemplation) as well as action in the world (praxis). When these two elements are separated, both the life and the mission of the church are deeply affected. Contemplation without action is an escape from concrete reality; action without contemplation is activism lacking a transcendent meaning. True spirituality requires a missionary contemplation and a contemplative mission.[6]

—René Padilla

Key Text: I Peter 2:9-12

But you are a chosen race, a royal priesthood, a holy nation, a people for his own possession, that you may proclaim the excellencies of him who called you out of darkness into his marvellous light. Once you were not a people, but now you are God's people; once you had not received mercy, but now you have received mercy. Beloved, I urge you as sojourners and exiles to abstain from the passions of the flesh, which wage war against your soul. Keep your conduct among the Gentiles honourable, so that when they speak against you as evildoers, they may see your good deeds and glorify God on the day of visitation.

Questions for Discussion

What are the components needed to form an authentic mission spirituality?

What deficiencies, at the level of spirituality, are churches seeking to remedy in our time?

What is the right balance between inner life and outward action for effective missionary engagement?

PRAYER

Praise be to you, O God, for the outpouring of your Holy Spirit,
bringing me the touch of your presence and the power of your life.
Forgive me, Lord, that I am often superficial in my faith,
easily distracted and content to remain in the shallows.
Grant me the courage, gracious Father, to launch out into the deep,
to pray with fervour and expectation, seeking your will.
Enable your church to grow in faith and spiritual maturity,
so as to have the integrity which will make its message ring true.
All for your glory and praise, in Christ's name. Amen

4

Mission and Power

TWENTY CENTURIES OF HISTORY

The first followers of Jesus were not by any stretch of the imagination a powerful group of people. On the contrary, they were drawn from the lower social strata of an occupied country in an obscure backwater of the Roman Empire. The idea that their movement would outlast that mighty Empire would have seemed laughable to most folk at the time. Yet to this unlikely community Jesus gave the promise that they would receive "power" when the Holy Spirit came upon them (Acts 1:8).

The question is: what kind of power was intended and how does it relate to the power exercised by political authorities? This question became an acute one for Christians after their faith was adopted by the Roman Empire following Constantine's declaration in its favour in 312. This marked the beginning of "Christendom", the alliance of church and state which was to define Europe for more than a thousand years. Though this has often been represented as a triumph for Christianity, was the church drawn into the politics of domination and repression which would undermine what it stands for in terms of the exercise of power?

In modern times, the Western world took the opportunity to extend the influence of Christendom to many different parts of the world. The mission of the church was closely linked to imperial and colonial expansion. Indeed, it has even been suggested that Christianity was the inspiration of Western civilisation's lust and will to dominate. For the indigenous population of many countries this meant that they were subject to violence at the physical, mental, emotional and spiritual levels. As Western powers imposed their rule around the world, did Christianity collude in the exercise of this kind of power?

THE CASE OF CANADA

In this chapter we consider the case of Canada. As in many situations worldwide, in modern times the indigenous people encountered newcomers who brought new technology, new cultural values and a new faith—Christianity. Initially, the treaties which European settlers made with the indigenous people promised friendship and a mutually beneficial relationship. However, as immigration increased and the settlers needed more and more land, attitudes hardened. By the mid-19th century, the British Government was speaking of the need to "civilise the Indian" and began its efforts to assimilate the indigenous people.

These initiatives were experienced by the indigenous people as a violent assault on their identity and values. Not only did they lose land and economic opportunity, they also experienced the systematic denigration of their culture and the imposition of alien norms. Closely involved in this process were the Christian churches. Arriving with the immigrant European community they shared its aspirations and values. This influenced the churches in their engagement with the indigenous people. They adapted themselves to a situation where political, economic and cultural power lay with a colonising power.

Once there was this little old woman and this little old man living in a beautiful house. One day a person from another place came to visit and they welcomed him into their home. He stayed and stayed until one day some of his relatives came also. They stayed. These visitors kept inviting more people to the house until finally the old man and woman were living on the veranda because there was no more room inside. The visitors occupied the whole house. The old man and woman kept saying to themselves 'when are these people going to leave so we can move back into our house?' Then another group of relatives of the first visitors arrived and the old man and woman were pushed off the veranda into the bog surrounding the house.[7]

MISSION THROUGH RESIDENTIAL SCHOOLS IN CANADA

A key part of the plan to assimilate the indigenous people was the establishment of residential schools, usually run by one of the churches. Children were removed from their families at an early age and placed in residential schools. The aim was that they would grow up under the influence of "modern" values and away from the supposedly depraved influence of their own families and communities. As one church leader put it, children were to be "caught young to be saved from what is on the whole the degenerating influence of their home environment".[8] Few in the churches challenged this understanding. Students were made to feel ashamed of their own cultural background and were schooled in the supposed superiority of "white" culture and values.

Terry LeBlanc, a *Mi'kmaq*/Acadian, from *Listuguj* First Nation, sets out the change in values which formed the aim of the residential schools:

1) Adopt European ideas of material value and wealth connected to resources of the land.

2) Accept the growing social-liberal way of life with autonomous personal well-being and individual competitiveness.
3) Sever connection to belief that the totality of creation is possessed of a spiritual nature.[9]

The churches and the state worked together along these lines in a massive effort to colonise the minds of the indigenous people. Receiving the gospel of Christ was presented as part and parcel of rejecting one's ancestral culture and assimilating to European norms and values. Mission and power came together in a way which was disastrous for the people on the receiving end. Remarkably, many of them have received the gospel and been baptised, finding in Jesus one who fulfils their ancestral faith. Today their Christian faith serves to underline their sense that they have suffered a great wrong.

The suffering inflicted by the residential schools was compounded by the fact that they were often under-funded and poorly run. Moreover, abundant evidence sadly shows that staff of the schools often abused their power. It was common for children to be physically, emotionally and sexually abused. For the indigenous people the residential schools represent a terrifying assault upon their identity and well-being. Despite growing awareness of the damage being done, the schools continued well into the 20th century with the last school being closed in 1998. By that time the indigenous people had undergone a profound social trauma which manifested itself in alcoholism, suicide, violence and ongoing sexual abuse.

Forgiveness and Reconciliation

Though it came late, by the late 20th century the churches became aware that they had been involved in something deeply wrong. Ian Morrison, a Presbyterian minister, describes how he came to be aware of the reality of the situation: "In all my years of ministry, I had never realized how cultural dominance had been so devastating to Aboriginal peoples. And an education model sponsored by my church had led to one of the most horrendous events in Canadian history. This realization forever changed my life."[10]

In a formal ceremony in 1982, the United Church of Canada chose these words for its Moderator to express repentance and to ask for forgiveness:

> Long before my people journeyed to this land your people were here, and you received from your elders an understanding of creation, and of the Mystery that surrounds us all that was deep, and rich and to be treasured.
>
> We did not hear you when you shared your vision. In our zeal to tell you the good news of Jesus Christ we were closed to the value of your spirituality.
>
> We confused western ways and culture with the depth and breadth and length and height of the Gospel of Christ.
>
> We imposed our civilization as a condition of accepting the Gospel.
>
> We tried to make you like us and in doing so we helped to destroy the vision that made you what you were. As a result, you, and we, are poorer and the image of the Creator in us is twisted, blurred and we are not what we are meant by God to be.
>
> We ask you to forgive us and to walk together with us in the spirit of Christ so that our peoples may be blessed and God's creation healed.[11]

For the indigenous people who were present in large numbers, this was a profound moment. They felt that they were finally released from the suffocating oppression which they had suffered for so long. There was dancing, crying and singing around the sacred fire to the beat of the drums. Finally, the people were free to cherish their heritage and express their identity, in the context of professing faith in Christ.

The movement of confession, repentance and forgiveness also found expression in restitution as churches sought to offer recompense to those who had suffered in the residential schools. Though admitting that they could never fully make good the psychological damage which had been done, the churches recognised their responsibility for the abuse of power and offered both acknowledgement and financial compensation. As a result, today there are new possibilities in terms of the relationship between indigenous people and Canadians descended from immigrants.

Wendy Fletcher, Principal and Dean at Vancouver School of Theology tells this story:

> On October 9th, 2008, I travelled to the Nisga'a village of Laxgalts'ap. I made the journey to attend the funeral of Bradley Martin, son of Willard Martin, Vancouver School of Theology alumnus and Nisga'a hereditary chief. Bradley had ended his own life. Over a century before, Christian missionaries, bringing their own worldview to this community, had insisted there be no proper burials when death is by suicide. The Nisga'a adopted and followed that teaching ever since, even as the church changed its thinking and practice. Willard insisted on giving his son the dignity of a Christian burial and settlement feast; I went to support him in his courage and his wisdom, and to honour the life of his son. Willard, as with many of his people, has survived the trauma of residential schooling and all the dislocation it engendered for so many. I carried with me the weight of our history, a colonizing church, a legacy of harm. I felt shame.
>
> When I arrived, Willard cautioned that likely very few would attend the funeral, as it was breaking with cultural practice. He then asked me to participate in the liturgy which would honour his son. Surprisingly, hundreds of Nisga'a came. When the

Eucharist was celebrated, every single person came forward to receive. When the Nisga'a priest, James, asked me to walk with him ahead of the casket to the graveside, I looked back. Ten young Nisga'a men carried their friend, refusing to put him down until the grave was reached. With tears streaming down their faces they walked and walked; behind them hundreds of Bradley's people walked with him his last mile. We stood around the open grave and then James turned and handed me his prayer book, 'You commit him to God for us', he said. As I said the words of committal, and we all stood there suffering and hoping together past the stain of an incredibly wounding history, I saw the healing of God begin. I saw the healing water of God's grace pour out to all corners of the earth and understood that nothing was beyond its reach.[12]

MISSION SUSPICIOUS OF POWER

Through experiences like the Canadian one Christians have learned the hard way that they need to be suspicious about the exercise of power. Such is human life that one group will always try to dominate another and these efforts are strengthened through religious legitimation. Hence the church always has to resist the lure of power. Many benefits come from being close to power, but they come at too high a price. When Christians allow their gospel to become implicated in the coercive use of power they always compromise the message. The use of force to promote a particular agenda and the infliction of suffering on innocent people can never present an authentic picture of Jesus Christ and his salvation. A colonising approach can never demonstrate the kind of power which is found in the gospel.

Belatedly, Christians have learned, from a mass of evidence gathered from many different parts of the world, that sharing the gospel with another community does not mean imposing new cultural values on them. Rather, mission means enabling people to bring all the riches of their cultural heritage to their reception of the gospel. When it is imposed by force the gospel loses its flavour. When it is embraced freely and interpreted in terms of the receiving culture it comes alive and does its work. Love, humility and solidarity rather than aggression, violence and domination are the notes to be struck in authentic Christian mission.

Meanwhile, the traumatic Canadian story brings the amazing assurance that when we do misappropriate and misuse power, the gospel brings healing, reconciliation and hope. As Wendy Fletcher concludes; "It appears that the witness of the Canadian church in this generation is that there is no harm beyond the reach of God's healing grace. All around us in these hours, the signs of a new world struggling to be born paint themselves across the backdrop of former desolations. Perhaps struggle is another word for hope. Mercy abounds and deliverance remakes us."[13]

KEY TEXT: I CORINTHIANS 12:14-26

For the body does not consist of one member but of many. If the foot should say, "Because I am not a hand, I do not belong to the body", that would not make it any less a part of the body. And if the ear should say, "Because I am not an eye, I do not belong to the body", that would not make it any less a part of the body. If the whole body were an eye, where would be the sense of hearing? If the whole body were an ear, where would be the sense of smell? But as it is, God arranged the members in the body, each one of them, as he chose. If all were a single member, where would the body be? As it is, there are many parts yet one body.

The eye cannot say to the hand, "I have no need of you", nor again the head to the feet, "I have no need of you." On the contrary, the parts of the body that seem to be weaker are indispensable, and on those parts of the body that we think less honourable we bestow the greater honour, and our unpresentable parts are treated with greater modesty, which our more presentable parts do not require. But God has so composed the body, giving greater honour to the parts that lacked it, that there may be no division in the body, but that the members may have the same care for one another. If one member suffers, all suffer together; if one member is honoured, all rejoice together.

QUESTIONS FOR DISCUSSION

What does Paul's analogy of the body have to teach us about a Christian understanding of power?

What happens when the churches become complicit in attempts to impose new cultural values on local people?

How should Christian mission position itself in relation to political, social and economic power?

PRAYER

I praise you, O God, that in the gospel of Jesus Christ there is power,
to bring me salvation and to transform the world.
Forgive me that I have valued the wrong kind of power,
power which means repression, suffering and despair for many of your children.
Expose, O God, all the ways in which I collude in unjust domination,
and grant me repentance, that I may turn away from every wrong use of power.
Help me to say "no" to alliance with all forms of domination and oppression,
and grant me the courage to live out the power of love every day.
For the sake of Christ the Lord. Amen

5

Christian Mission among Other Faiths

COMING TO TERMS WITH PLURALITY

How to regard other religions and how to relate to people of a different faith—these are among the most searching questions faced by anyone exploring the meaning of Christian mission today. The confident expectation of Edinburgh 1910 that other religions would melt away in face of the triumphant advance of Christianity has clearly been disappointed. The 20th century did indeed see Christian advance in many parts of the world, but parallel to this was renewal and expansion within other major religions as well. Contrary to the expectations of those who thought the world would become more secular, we have entered an age of religious renewal. One result of this is that, as a matter of fact, the permanent make-up of the world community includes a number of religions. However we may assess it, we have to come to terms with plurality in regard to religion.

Christians of all persuasions have been coming to terms with this reality. Witness to Jesus Christ is offered in a world where many belong to other religions. Gone is the day when it was possible to speak of a "Christian world" and a "Non-Christian world". Christians are found in every part of the world and so too are adherents of other faiths. The question is: what sort of interaction is to be recommended?

Built into Christianity is a missionary mandate which ensures that Christians aspire to share their faith with others, including those who belong to other religions. No less essential to Christianity is the command to love our neighbours, particularly if they are different from ourselves, so there is a strong basis for a positive relationship with people of other faiths. How to build mutually supportive and constructive relationships with people of other faiths—fulfilling the love commandment—while at the same time commending Jesus as Saviour—fulfilling the evangelistic mandate—is a deeply challenging question.

RELIGIONS IN A GLOBALISED WORLD

The relations of the different religions today are not formed in a world which is free of political and economic influences. The constellation of political and economic power described as "globalisation" shapes inter-religious encounter everywhere. There are powerful centres within the world economy which extend their influence far and wide, strengthening some while marginalising others, as well as creating new opportunities for developing more positive relationships.

At the cross-section of global and local influences sharp questions of identity arise. Often people draw on their religious tradition to answer these questions. In this way religious identity becomes one of the most pressing, as well as one of the most conflictive, issues in many contexts. Inter-religious relations are considered not in tranquillity but amidst desperate life-and-death struggles fomented by the most powerful political and economic forces of our time. In countries like Indonesia, India, Israel and Palestine, people of different faiths lived together peacefully for many years and quite suddenly found that their religious identity was the defining factor in deadly inter-communal strife. New and powerful forces had entered their situation—globalisation was taking effect in divisive and destructive ways.

Another major trend, driven by globalisation is the movement of people to cities. More than 50% of the world's population now live in cities and this percentage is rising every year. One outcome of urbanisation is that people belonging to different religious traditions are thrown together and have to learn to share physical and social space. Migration brings religious believers from distant places as well as from nearby, making the religious complexion of many cities more plural than anything we have known before. Some170 million people, 3% of the world's population, are migrants. In contrast to 1910 when most migrants were Europeans settling in the "colonies", today the movement is in the opposite direction. Often driven by the forces of poverty or conflict, migrants from Asia, Africa, the Middle East and Latin America come to find a new life in the Global North. In the process, they bring an unprecedented degree of religious plurality to the cities of Europe and North America. Often vulnerable, their faith may be strengthened by the migrant experience.

For aboriginal or indigenous peoples, globalisation can often present itself as a threatening force. Where market forces are decisive there tends to be little consideration for the traditional culture which forms the identity of an indigenous people group. Religious faith is commonly a matter of great importance to such groups. Many have embraced the Christian faith but seek to interpret it in terms of their own history and culture. Others maintain their own "primal" religion or profess one of the other world religions. Often they draw on religious resources in the effort to sustain their life and identity in face of hostile forces of globalisation.

At the other end of the spectrum, many benefit from globalisation and new technology, exploiting fresh opportunities. New communities are formed through the internet. Sometimes called "virtual" communities, these are reference groups which interact online. Among the many possibilities for encounter, this new communication technology introduces possibilities for adherents of different religious traditions to engage with one another. Websites for inter-religious dialogue or for collaboration on issues of common concern are being created in great profusion. In this way people of different faiths who are far apart physically are encountering one another and having opportunity to engage one another at the religious level.

DIVERSITY OF APPROACH

Christians have responded to this new situation in a variety of ways. The question of how to understand other faiths and how to relate to their adherents has been a contested one. During the 20th century, different approaches found favour at different times:

- Edinburgh 1910 was much influenced by fulfilment theory. This is an approach which affirms other religions but sees them reaching their fulfilment in Jesus Christ. Hinduism or African Traditional Religion, e.g., are viewed as equivalents of the Old Testament, preparing the way for the coming of Christ in which they find their fulfilment.
- The influential Laymen's Inquiry into Christian mission, published in 1932, went further in arguing that missionaries should work on the basis of a positive assessment of other religions. Rather than

denouncing or seeking to supplant other religions, missionaries should regard themselves as co-workers with proponents of other faiths. Hendrik Kraemer, a Dutch mission thinker, took the discussion in a different direction in 1938 when he published The Christian Message in a Non-Christian World. He argued that God's revelation in Jesus Christ is so entirely different from other religions that there is no possibility of the latter leading to the former or of "points of contact" being identified.

- In the second half of the 20th century the influence of Vatican II among Roman Catholics and of the World Council of Churches among Protestants promoted a much more positive assessment of other religions. Dialogue, based on mutual recognition and mutual respect, became the favoured approach. This positive approach to other faiths was developed by some thinkers into a move away from the finality or superiority of Jesus Christ towards a recognition of the independent validity of all religions. Crossing the "theological Rubicon", some embraced a pluralist theology where there are different ways to God.

- For others, dialogue was suspected of involving a compromise of the faith and pluralist theology was thought to undermine the unique claims of Christ on which Christian faith is based. A renewed emphasis was placed on proclamation as the key element in Christian witness, with the aim of conversion: people becoming Christians and departing from their earlier faith.

- Another recent approach has been described as the "dialogue of life". The focus is not on religious differences but on engaging together with the issues of life in a particular context. Understanding grows through sharing in analysis and action on relevant issues while all participants maintain the integrity of their particular faith.

THE SPIRITUAL DIMENSION

Renewed consideration of the work of the Holy Spirit has opened up new perspectives on the relation of Christian faiths and other faiths. The Orthodox Churches carry a deep awareness of the work of the Spirit in sustaining communion between God and the entire created order. The Roman Catholic Church has been open to the possibility that the Holy Spirit works through other religions to lead people to salvation in Jesus Christ. This opens up a large discussion about the ways in which the Holy Spirit carries out this work. Certain Pentecostals have been alert to the power of the Holy Spirit working among people professing other faiths. On the basis that a spiritual dimension exists in all religions, Pentecostals view this as a sphere where the Holy Spirit is active. The dynamics of the interaction between the Holy Spirit and the spirits active in a particular context constitute a dimension of inter-religious encounter which may open up more opportunities for inter-religious understanding and cooperation than a merely intellectual approach.

The amazing growth of Christianity in Africa over the past century has been attributed to the openness of Africans to life's spiritual dimension—a key feature of the "primal religion" which has pervasive influence throughout the continent. In particular, the spectacular growth of charismatic and Pentecostal Christianity in Africa is thought to be based on the resonance between the emphases of Pentecostalism and the traditional African worldview. The unseen world of the spirits, on this understanding, is no less present and influential than the material world. Pentecostalism is geared to work at this level, more a matter of experience than of rational thought. It brings power to restore harmony at the individual, community and cosmic levels. This may sometimes involve a "power encounter" in which the Holy Spirit demonstrates the power of Christ to defeat rival spiritual forces.

INTEGRITY AND OPENNESS

To have integrity as a Christian means being ever conscious of commitment to mission. You are called to bear witness to Jesus Christ in all that you say and do. Whoever you may encounter, whether or not they belong to another faith, you owe it to them to share your faith and conviction with them by your presence, your words and your action. This, however, is not to say that you should fulfil this responsibility in a way which is arrogant or aggressive. On the contrary, the responsibility will be fulfilled much more faithfully and effectively if it is approached in a spirit of mutual respect and love.

Dialogue does not have to mean that you compromise your own convictions. In fact, it provides an opportunity for you to share your most cherished convictions so long as you are equally willing to listen to the sincerely held convictions of your dialogue partner. Listening is at least as important as speaking in the communication of the gospel of Christ. The two-way exchange which dialogue entails provides an ideal opportunity for this to take place. It is a natural expression of the good neighbourliness which is expected of every Christian.

It is always demanding to encounter someone who is "other", quite different from ourselves and our experience. Yet it is in such encounters that we are most likely to grow and expand our horizons. It can be a big struggle to overcome stereotypes and even the demonising of others, but we are always the better for it. The biblical stress on good neighbourliness and hospitality underpins an approach which seeks to understand the "other" as fully as possible. Can authentic Christian love do anything less?

This kind of dialogue is less a studied procedure for inter-faith encounter and more a way of life in which our good neighbourliness ensures that we aim to understand our neighbours as fully as possible, as well as sharing our life and convictions with them. Joining with neighbours of other faiths in community projects for peace, human rights, social activities, health improvement, political freedom and democracy is an important aspect of being in dialogue with them. As we express gospel values in our context we are drawn into deepening relationships and dialogue becomes a very natural way of life. It is a sobering reality about the lifestyle of Christians that relatively few have ever had a serious conversation about faith with someone from another religion. The converse is also true: relatively few adherents of other religions have had an opportunity to hear about Christian belief from someone whom they know and trust. The more authentic dialogue which takes place, the better the people of the world will understand one another and the fuller will be the fulfilment of mission responsibility on the part of Christians.

> We cannot point to any other way of salvation than Jesus Christ. At the same time we cannot set limits to God's saving power.... We appreciate this tension, and do not attempt to solve it
>
> —World Council of Churches, San Antonio, 1989
>
> While everyone has a right to invite others to an understanding of their faith, it should not be exercised by violating others' rights and religious sensibilities.
>
> —World Council of Churches, Toward a Code of Conduct on Conversion, 2006

Like Paul at the Areopagus in Athens, Christians enter into dialogue in the expectation that God is already present in the life and experience of those they encounter. This radical openness, however, is held in tension with our conviction that something quite extraordinary has occurred in the life, death and resurrection of Jesus Christ. The "scandal of particularity" at the heart of Christian faith is that in this event God meets us and saves us in a unique way. To set aside or to soften this claim would be to strike at the core of Christian belief. Yet it is important to remember that Christianity itself, as well as every other faith, has to be constantly challenged by the radical nature of what God has done in Jesus Christ.

It is also important to remember that God is present and active in all the world and in all of history. Without detracting from the special character of God's action in Jesus Christ we can be aware that "there's a wideness in God's mercy" which extends to every context and every people. The way in which the offer of salvation reaches people is God's business. Meanwhile, our task is to bear witness to the unique reality of Jesus Christ, both proclaiming with clarity and entering into dialogue with sensitivity.

KEY TEXT: ACTS 17:22-28

So Paul, standing in the midst of the Areopagus, said: "Men of Athens, I perceive that in every way you are very religious. For as I passed along and observed the objects of your worship, I found also an altar with this inscription, 'To the unknown god.' What therefore you worship as unknown, this I proclaim to you. The God who made the world and everything in it, being Lord of heaven and earth, does not live in temples made by man, nor is he served by human hands, as though he needed anything, since he himself gives to all mankind life and breath and everything. And he made from one man every nation of mankind to live on all the face of the earth, having determined allotted periods and the boundaries of their dwelling place, that they should seek God in the hope that they might feel their way towards him and find him. Yet he is actually not far from each one of us, for 'In him we live and move and have our being'; as even some of your own poets have said, 'For we are indeed his offspring.'"

QUESTIONS FOR DISCUSSION

What approach did the apostle Paul take to other religions?

What is your assessment of the value of engaging with other religious traditions (a) on intellectual terms, (b) in terms of the "dialogue of life", and (c) on spiritual terms?

What opportunities and what obstacles face us today when we seek to relate to adherents of other religions in an authentically Christian way?

PRAYER

Praise be to you, O God, for the work of your Spirit,
active everywhere and among all people.
Thank you for the good news about Jesus Christ and your command
that it be shared with people everywhere.
Open my heart, I ask, that I may draw close to people of other faiths,
to respect, to listen, to learn, to grow, to act together.
Grant that I might have the love and sensitivity,
to faithfully witness to Jesus Christ by my life, my words, my actions,
that your gracious purposes might be fulfilled, even through me.
For the sake of Jesus Christ, Saviour and Lord. Amen

6

A New Frontier for Mission: Postmodernity

Modernity, the view of life which arose from the intellectual movement known as the Enlightenment, is characterised by a high level of confidence in the power of human reason. Through the exercise of our reason it is expected that we will be able to offer comprehensive and conclusive explanations of reality. Modernity was a prevailing ideology, at least among Europeans and North Americans, from the late 18th until the late 20th centuries. Their global power during this period has ensured that few parts of the world are unaffected.

Today we are aware that ways of thinking have emerged which suggest that we have entered a world of thought which comes *after* modernity. It has important elements of continuity with modernity but is also, in significant ways, a rejection of modernity. Though it is an imprecise term, "postmodernity" has come to be used as a summary word for this new intellectual and cultural environment.

For postmodernity there are no grand, objective narratives which provide a comprehensive explanation of reality. This aspect of modernity has been discredited by its expression in political ideologies such as Communism or Nazism and by the way in which a theory of the superiority of the white race was used to sustain oppressive colonialism and imperialism in much of the world during the 19th and 20th centuries. The catastrophic political events of the twentieth century, particularly the two World Wars caused by events in Europe, shattered Western optimism and self-confidence. This collapse of confidence in the vision of modernity left in its wake a profound distrust in grand, universal theories.

Confidence in the exercise of pure reason has also been shaken. At the heart of modernity was confidence in the power of the scientific method to create solutions to every problem. Today it is recognised that everyone's analysis is influenced by their own interests and their quest to advance their own power. There is a profound distrust of authority. No point of view is superior to any other. The individual is free to pick and choose according to their own taste and requirements. Those who hold power are distrusted and particular suspicion is directed towards hierarchical and authoritarian structures.

With its strong confidence in the power of rationality and scientific ingenuity to solve human problems, modernity engendered optimism about the future. Though there may be occasional setbacks, the overall sense is of being part of a grand project which is triumphantly advancing. In contrast, postmodernity has no belief that the future will be better than the present. Change has to be navigated, but not with any confidence that it is necessarily making things better.

Recognition of plurality is essential to the postmodern vision. Many cultural, linguistic, political, religious and other options exist simultaneously. The individual may choose the understanding of things and the way of life preferred at the moment. An eclectic approach is favoured, so each individual can construct their own personal understanding of reality. Change is constant so identity is constantly in flux and our understanding of the world has to be continually renegotiated. Contextuality is pivotal to postmodernity. Your understanding is determined by the perspective from which you approach the question. There is no such thing as an objective view. All human knowledge is partial and biased. Beauty is in the eye of the beholder.

The Influence of Postmodernity

No one should underestimate the pervasive influence of postmodernity. It permeates whole cultures, shaping the way that people think and live. It has shifted the paradigm on the basis of which people understand themselves and their lives. Even people who would never use the term "postmodern" to describe themselves can often be greatly influenced by this way of thinking.

How do you know the truth?
Pre-modern people would reply, "I've been told." They depend on authority and tradition.

Modern people would reply, "I think." They depend on reason and scientific method.

Postmodern people would reply, "I feel." They depend on subjective emotions and experiences.

Where is authority to be found?
Pre-modern people would reply, "God is the author of life and through religion we know God's will."

Modern people would reply, "Reason is the final authority, enabling us to understand the forces of nature and the flow of history."

Postmodern people would reply, "I am the author of my own life and I choose the perspectives which I need to create its meaning."

Some have questioned whether postmodernity is as extensive and enduring as its advocates claim. It is pointed out that in today's world there is a widespread religious awakening which tends to promote a return to traditional views and values. However, the decision to adopt a traditional, or even fundamentalist, position can be seen as a matter of choice, a personal rejection of dominant notions and habits, and therefore as an expression of postmodernity. While postmodernity holds sway among affluent and urbanised populations, particularly in the North, it appears that it has little resonance with poor and rural populations, particularly in the Global South. Nonetheless, given the power of postmodernity in centres of power and in the media through which these centres extend their influence, its influence is wide and pervasive. It shapes the thinking and action even of those who are hostile to its premises.

HOT ISSUES IN A POSTMODERN SOCIETY

Consideration of postmodernity raises some key issues from a Christian point of view:

- Postmodernity has heightened our awareness of "otherness" and of our relationships with others. Yet does it provide resources to make for healthy relationships, especially as people become more distant from one another, often depending on the virtual communities of the internet?
- The relationship between believing and belonging is a contested one. Some have suggested that in postmodern societies people believe without belonging—holding the essential tenets of Christianity without feeling

the need to join the institutional church. Others have identified the opposite trend where people belong without believing—maintaining connection with the institutional church but without believing in Christ in any meaningful way.

- Another contested area is that of freedom of speech and the requirements of tolerance. Postmodernity is extremely sensitive to discrimination on grounds of such identifiers as gender, ethnicity, religion or sexual orientation. Canons of "political correctness" specify the language to be used to express the correct attitude. Where a religious tradition contravenes these canons its proponents can be exposed to much hostility—which can lead them to question whether their freedom of religion and freedom of speech are being upheld.

- The ethics of conversion are very much under scrutiny in a postmodern context. There is suspicion of coercion and improper use of power. On the other hand, freedom to choose is highly prized and radical conversion may be more viable than has been the case in many other social contexts.

- Since postmodernity emphases change without progress, how is it possible to have meaningful hope in regard to the future? If the human condition is such that it needs hope to supply the needed motivation, where is such hope going to come from?

POSTMODERN CHRISTIANITY?

There are clear signs that the pervasive influence of postmodernity extends to Christianity itself. In the Western world where the influence of postmodernity is strongest, it is possible to detect significant changes in the prevailing understanding of Christianity. In its earlier history Christianity put great emphasis on doctrine, expressing itself in sharp, clear propositional statements. Today the emphasis is on experience—the practice of the faith. This has been described as a "softer" Christianity, with the emphasis on life and ethics rather than faith and doctrine. Dialogue is preferred to proclamation. Aesthetic beauty is considered more important than theological accuracy. An inclusive rather than an exclusive approach is taken to those adhering to other religions and worldviews. This shift is in tune with postmodern subjectivity and scepticism towards absolutes.

In making this shift is Christianity selling out to an alien philosophy? It might seem as if there is a head-on clash here. Essential to Christianity is belief in the existence of absolute truth and confidence that it is found in Christ. Yet notes of uncertainty and provisionality about absolutes can be detected in the New Testament. "For now we see in a mirror dimly," says the apostle Paul (I Corinthians 13:12). The truth is there, but our perceptions of it are limited and fragmented. On this basis can Christians be content to operate on a postmodern basis where no one can claim a position of certainty but where we may dialogue together with a view to resolving differences and working towards common goals?

This question becomes particularly acute in relation to salvation. From a postmodern standpoint, the traditional Christian affirmation that "outside of the church there is no salvation" appears arrogant and intolerant. However, the New Testament understanding of the relationship between the church and salvation appears to have a fluid quality. Perhaps postmodernity, with its emphasis on life and experience rather than on structures and membership, is in some ways closer to the New Testament understanding of the church than are some of the more traditional Christian positions?

Nonetheless, it is clear that belonging to Christ is not a solitary preoccupation. It necessarily involves associating with others who belong to Christ, in the fellowship of the church. In a postmodern context the virtue of belonging to the church may be advocated without the need to harshly condemn alternative options which are chosen by others. While Christians may have confidence in baptism and church membership as the normal way of salvation, they must recognise that salvation is the prerogative of God. Humility is the appropriate attitude in relating to those who have chosen other paths.

Christian mission is regarded with suspicion in the postmodern context. It can easily appear to have a coercive approach—seeking to impose itself uninvited. In this context, it is clearer than ever that actions speak louder than words. Living a life which authentically represents Jesus Christ is more likely to gain a favourable response. Engaging in actions for justice or for the care of creation can open the way to meaningful encounter and discussion.

> The Chinese character "sheng", signifying "holy", consists of three parts: there is a large ear and a small mouth, posing above the character for "responsibility". Could this be a fruitful metaphor for Christian mission in a postmodern environment? The large ear and small mouth signify responsible, respectful proclamation and intellectually honest dialogue, combined with earnest efforts to listen and to understand.[14]

There are clear points of dissonance between the Christian vision and that of postmodernity. Whereas for postmodernity there can be no one big story which accounts for everything, Christians find the clue to understanding all of our reality in what is revealed in Jesus Christ. Nonetheless, postmodernity brings constructive challenges to Christianity and helps it to discover aspects of its message which have been neglected. Though in some respects there is mutual challenge between a Christian worldview and a postmodern one, in other respects there is strong resonance between the two.

MISSION IN A POSTMODERN CONTEXT

As in any new situation, Christian mission has to relate itself to the surrounding culture. In the case of postmodernity this must involve recognising the virtues and strengths which it represents as well as discerning its destructive elements. The following are suggested as points where there may be constructive Christian engagement with postmodernity.

Distrust of power is so strong in postmodernity that there is a reluctance to take on the responsibilities of leadership. Does this provide an opportunity for the churches to demonstrate attractive models of leadership? Hierarchical or authoritarian models are unlikely to commend themselves. However, the servant leadership which was such a distinctive quality of Jesus' ministry may offer to postmodern societies a pattern of leadership which is attractive and compelling. The question is: how consistently does the church demonstrate this model?

Christians always have to strike a balance between theory and practice in the way they express their faith. In the postmodern context, credibility comes less from doctrinal clarity and more from a life consistent with one's convictions and the ability to encourage, enrich and guide others. Academic proficiency carries less weight than spiritual authenticity when it comes to have a cutting edge in the postmodern context. Can patterns of formation in the church adapt to this reality?

Another aspect of postmodernity which may be ripe for engagement by Christian mission is its lack of confidence about the future. In the context of the multifaceted economic and ecological crisis facing today's world it seems that postmodernity finds it impossible to discover any note of hope. Christians, on the other hand, are geared to the future and inspired by hope. Moreover, they use the transformation for which they hope as a lever to advance positive change here and now in the present.

Today's environmental crisis presents a particular challenge. Modernity stands discredited, among other things, because of its exploitative approach to the earth's resources. Postmodernity seeks a more holistic approach and greater sympathy with the natural order. Christians have an opportunity here to engage with today's most pressing questions. They may have to acknowledge that the churches have done little to protect the environment. Indeed, they have been cheerleaders for the advance of the modernity which has caused so much damage to the environment. However, the widespread rediscovery today of the biblical understanding of stewardship of creation is something that speaks directly to a central concern of postmodernity.

Key Text: Acts 10:44-48

> While Peter was still saying these things, the Holy Spirit fell on all who heard the word. And the believers from among the circumcised who had come with Peter were amazed, because the gift of the Holy Spirit was poured out even on the Gentiles. For they were hearing them speaking in tongues and extolling God. Then Peter declared, "Can anyone withhold water for baptizing these people, who have received the Holy Spirit just as we have?" And he commanded them to be baptized in the name of Jesus Christ. Then they asked him to remain for some days.

Questions for Discussion

What kind of experience leads people to believe and be baptised?

What points do Christianity and postmodernity have in common and at what points are there clear divergences between the two?

What would be the main features of a mission strategy to communicate the good news of Jesus Christ to people whose thinking is shaped by postmodernity?

PRAYER

I praise you, O God, for the diversity of the earth and its peoples,
and for how much we have to learn from one another.
Grant that I may have humility to listen and courage to speak,
so that today's questions would deepen my faith and understanding.
I thank you that the good news of Jesus Christ gains clarity
as it crosses new frontiers and meets new worlds of thought.
Let me live, O God, in a way which mirrors the character of Jesus
my Saviour,
and may my witness ring true both to friend and stranger.
For the sake of Jesus Christ your Son. Amen

7

Education and Formation for Mission

MISSION AND THEOLOGICAL EDUCATION

Ongoing exploration of the meaning of the faith is very closely related to the mission of the church. For the sake of its maturity, mission engagement needs to be subject to thought and analysis. For the sake of its relevance, theological thinking needs to be informed and challenged by mission engagement. Hence education, from the earliest days of Christianity, has been essential to the sustaining, defending and handing on of the faith.

At the heart of mission is the formation of the people who will be its exponents. In this, theological education has a vital role to play. Without the knowledge and the skills which effective theological education imparts, mission practitioners will lack depth and direction. Those with mission at heart therefore set high value on appropriate theological education.

The Edinburgh 1910 World Missionary Conference was a case in point. Great stress was laid on the importance of the theological formation of missionaries for their task. A strong vision emerged of churches and missionary societies cooperating in the development of common training programmes, with interdenominational institutions being envisaged in Shanghai, Madras, Calcutta, Beirut and Cairo. This vision was ground-breaking in several respects, since it proposed:

- theological education of missionaries outside the traditional centres of the North;
- a globally coordinated policy for development of theological education in the South;
- centralised and interdenominational institutions of theological education in the South;
- theological education on an advanced academic level.

Besides the theological formation of missionaries, Edinburgh 1910 also placed a major focus on the education of indigenous leadership for the emerging churches of the "mission fields" of the South. This included an emphasis on the importance of theological education being conducted in vernacular languages.

> We believe that the primary purpose to be served by the edu-
> cational work of missionaries is that of training of the native
> Church to bear its own proper witness .... We believe that the
> most important of all ends which missionary education ought
> to set itself to serve, is that of training those who are to be spiri-
> tual leaders and teachers of their own.[15]

—Conclusion of the Report of Commission III, Edinburgh 1910

The impetus from Edinburgh 1910 was carried forward by the International Missionary Council until it established the Theological Education Fund (TEF) in 1958. This had a huge impact in resourcing theological education worldwide. The vision of the TEF was to foster theological education characterised by:

- *quality* combining intellectual rigor, spiritual maturity, and commitment;
- *authenticity* involving critical encounter with each cultural context in the design, purpose and shape of theological education;

- *creativity*, understood as promoting new approaches in mission.[16]

The TEF initiative has done much to build up theological education in the Global South. It demonstrated that there is more to theology than absorbing models developed in the North. It has championed the contextual character of theology and thus provided a rich learning experience to the whole church. Its vision remains inspiring. The challenge is how to take it forward in the very different context of Christian mission in the 21st century.

NEW DIRECTIONS FOR THEOLOGICAL EDUCATION

The captivity of Northern theology to Enlightenment patterns of thought in modern times has often resulted in the dominance of a detached and decontextualised approach to the theological task. Academic credibility has sometimes been gained at the cost of faithful attention to the ministry and mission of the people of God in the world.

Particularly in the Global South, innovative, creative and mission-minded models of theological education are being developed. Without sacrificing academic integrity, these provide formation, discipleship and preparation for leadership for both lay people and those preparing for ordained ministry.

A major new development concerns gender. Although it is estimated that in 1910 55% of missionaries were women, it was men who overwhelmingly predominated in theological education. This has greatly changed in the course of 100 years. Today no one could miss the enormous contribution which women theologians have made to methodology, orientation and content across the theological curriculum. Yet much remains to be done, in many parts of the world, to enable and encourage gifted women to gain access to theological education and find their vocation in theological teaching and research. For the sake of gender justice and a more complete understanding of the faith, the contribution of women theologians is indispensable.

The advent of online education and e-learning has introduced exciting new possibilities for theological education. For the first time, Christians in different parts of the world can engage instantly with one another. Among the uses of digital technology in theological education are:

- web-based courses of study;
- research groups working via the internet;
- distance degree courses at all levels using digital formats;
- electronic library and other data resources.

Theological education by extension has long been recognised as a strategic means of equipping the whole church for ministry and mission. Digital technology provides unprecedented opportunity for high-quality theological education to be accessible to all who have an internet connection.

No longer is theological education the preserve of the clergy. The growth of the churches in the Global South has been so rapid that the emergence of new congregations has outmatched the capacity of the church to produce full-time pastors. Undaunted, congregations have generated their own leadership. Often these home-grown leaders have benefited immeasurably from courses of theological education by extension, usually run on very limited resources. The empowerment of the laity and broadened access to theological education now appears attractive to churches in the North which have gifted lay members and a shortage of clergy.

Great social forces of our time, such as migration and electronic communication, have brought the peoples of the world into contact with one another as never before. This opens up new possibilities for a dialogical approach to theological education. The conversation no longer needs to be in a restricted circle. In fact, theological understanding can be enhanced by engaging with others who bring different perspectives and new questions. Dialogue emerges as an inviting method for the task of doing theology.

A particularly important interface is found in the opportunities to engage those who profess other faiths. This can take place at a number of different levels:

- the dialogue of life, where people naturally relate to each other across religious boundaries in the course of their daily living;
- social dialogue, where people of various faiths collaborate with one another in the cause of peace and justice;
- intellectual dialogue, which can explore different beliefs and their claims to truth;
- spiritual dialogue, where people open themselves to the force of one another's religious experiences.[17]

The perspectives offered by this kind of engagement with other faiths must be allowed to fall across all parts of the theological task, not introduced as a specialist topic once the core curriculum has been completed.

> Dialogue does not require people to relinquish or alter their beliefs before entering into it; on the contrary, genuine dialogue demands that each partner brings to it the fullness of themselves and the tradition in which they stand. As they grow in mutual understanding they will be able to share more and more of what they bring with the other. Inevitably, both partners to the dialogue will be affected and changed by this process, for it is a mutual sharing.[18]
>
> —Lambeth Conference, 1998

Christians need to be equipped to engage in dialogue with people of all religions and with those who promote a secular worldview. However, at this time in history there is a premium on Christian–Muslim dialogue. The degree to which Christians and Muslims continue to misunderstand one another presents a major challenge to the theological task. To develop a constructive approach to Islam in the North it is vital that there is in-depth theological engagement. For the future of Christian minority churches in Muslim majority countries it is important that their leaders are equipped to enter into serious dialogue with Muslim counterparts. Both for world peace and for theological integrity, serious engagement with Islam must be at the heart of theological education today.

NEW NETWORKS

Given the speed of change and the number of new challenges which are presenting themselves in the field of theological education, there is need for stronger global networks to be developed. The Edinburgh 2010 process has broken new ground in bringing together representatives of historic, Evangelical, charismatic, Pentecostal and Independent churches to consider the development of theological education. Rather than being confined to restricted circles, great mutual strength can be drawn from such an expansive network.

There is need to reinvigorate efforts to strengthen theological education on a worldwide basis. How much could be achieved by churches with greater financial resources pooling their funds so as to create a resource base from which to work strategically for the development of theological education worldwide. Human and material resources could then be deployed where the need is greatest.

Regional associations, at their best, have been a great source of mutual strength. Today some would need to be reconstituted, taking account of a wider circle of institutions active in their area.

They can have an important enabling role in setting standards, generating appropriate resources and promoting excellence in their regions.

Another area ripe for renewal is the ecumenical approach to theological education. There is much to be gained from pooling the resources of a number of churches and creating an institution where students undergo their formation in an ecumenical context. This broadens their horizons and fosters ecumenical confidence. Much to be regretted is the fragmentation and denominational isolation which has been a feature of recent years in a number of different contexts. A pressing need to day is to revive interdenominational structures in theological education where they have faltered, and to create new ones on an even wider basis.

JUSTICE AND ACCESSIBILITY

The distribution of resources for theological education mirrors the imbalance in the global economy which provides some countries with abundant resources and others with great scarcity. The average full cost for one student place per year at Princeton Theological Seminary in the USA is approximately US$60,000, while the average cost for a BTh student place in an institution of theological education in Nepal is just US$1,000 per year. Little wonder that there is a brain drain from South to North when resources are so unequally distributed. Thoughtful Christians cannot look on this discrepancy with any degree of complacency.

The fast-growing churches of the Global South throw up a plethora of profound theological questions. They need suitably equipped institutions to address these questions in the light of the theology of the whole church. They need a theologically informed leadership to guide the rapidly expanding movement of faith of which they are part. Now is the time to take a global view and to share resources as may be necessary to ensure that access to theological education is available where it is needed.

In some respects it is an advantage to theological education worldwide that English has emerged as the dominant international language of theology. However, this brings the risk that national and vernacular languages are neglected as media of theological thinking and discussion. Theology really comes home when it can be discussed in the mother tongue. The diversity of language in which the Christian faith is expressed represents an enormous strength. This is something to cherish.

The welcome opportunity to share in worldwide discussion through a common international language, such as English, French or Spanish, needs to be balanced with the need for resources to be developed to foster the development of theology in vernacular languages. Both are essential if Christianity is to demonstrate and experience both its local and its global character.

We have seen that theological education is essential to the task of mission. The reverse also holds. A mission perspective is essential to the task of theological education. Since the theological curriculum of the North was formed at a time when Europe was largely absorbed with its own life, it had little mission perspective. It was concerned simply with understanding the faith which, at least nominally, everyone believed. So strong is the influence of that experience that mission remains a peripheral concern. It is often regarded as a specialist subject, somewhat detached from the core curriculum. Yet the need of the North today is for a missionary theology and every part of the curriculum needs to be infused with a mission perspective. On this pathway, so far, only a few tentative steps have been taken.

This may challenge models of theological education which privilege academic prowess at the expense of character formation and pastoral sensitivity. It is important for theology to be done in conversation with other academic disciplines and for students to meet recognised academic standards. Yet this needs to be balanced with the growth in faith and discipleship which the church rightly expects as the outcome of well-balanced theological education. How to strike the right balance is a challenging question today.

KEY TEXT: NEHEMIAH 8:1-8

And all the people gathered as one man into the square before the Water Gate. And they told Ezra the scribe to bring the Book of the Law of Moses that the Lord had commanded Israel. So Ezra the priest brought the Law before the assembly, both men and women and all who could understand what they heard, on the first day of the seventh month. And he read from it facing the square before the Water Gate from early morning until midday, in the presence of the men and women and those who could understand. And the ears of all the people were attentive to the Book of the Law. And Ezra the scribe stood on a wooden platform that they had made for the purpose. And beside him stood Mattithiah, Shema, Anaiah, Uriah, Hilkiah, and Maaseiah on his right hand, and Pedaiah, Mishael, Malchijah, Hashum, Hashbaddanah, Zechariah, and Meshullam on his left hand. And Ezra opened the book in the sight of all the people, for he was above all the people, and as he opened it all the people stood. And Ezra blessed the Lord, the great God, and all the people answered "Amen, Amen," lifting up their hands and worshipped the Lord with their faces to the ground. Also Jeshua, Bani, Sherebiah, Jamin, Akkub, Shabbethai, Hodiah, Maaseiah, Kelita, Azariah, Jozabad, Hanan, Pelaiah, the Levites, helped the people to understand the Law, while the people remained in their places. They read from the book, from the Law of God, clearly, and they gave the meaning, so that the people understood the reading.

QUESTIONS FOR DISCUSSION

Who should participate in theological education and how can such education be made accessible to all who need it?

How can a focus on mission help to reshape theological education in today's world?

What developments are most needed to make theological education relevant to our contemporary context?

PRAYER

I praise you, O God, that from you come all wisdom and all knowledge, and that you have spoken in Jesus Christ the word I most need to hear. Give me ears, I pray, to hear your word and a heart to understand, and grant me ambition that I may ever deepen my faith and understanding.

I thank you for all who commit their lives to theological education, and for the sacrificial effort which created theological institutions around the world.

May your Holy Spirit inspire those who learn and those who teach, that faith may be deepened and knowledge of your grace expanded. For the sake of Jesus Christ, teacher and Lord. Amen

8

Better Together: Mission and Unity

EDINBURGH 1910: MISSION MEANS UNITY

It is a striking historical fact that it was the people most immersed in worldwide mission who put the question of the unity of the church firmly on the agenda at the start of the 20th century. Edinburgh 1910 was a conference organised by the missionary societies and church mission boards which were active in evangelism all over the world. Their experience in mission had taught them a big lesson: unity is vital. This became a keynote of Edinburgh 1910.

In context after context, the message from missionaries on the ground was the same: so much more could be achieved if missions and churches could work more closely together. In fact, through working in a new culture, many had found that the differences between their denominations and societies began to look much smaller than before. Leaders of the emerging churches in the Global South added to the challenge by asking why they had to import the historic denominational divisions of the North.

> For the achievement of the ultimate and highest end of all missionary work—the establishment in these non-Christian lands of Christ's one Church—real unity must be attained.[19]
>
> —Report of Commission VIII, Edinburgh 1910

A head of steam built up which propelled into the 20th century a new dynamic, usually described as the ecumenical movement. Following the devastating setback of the First World War, the missionary movement regrouped in 1921 to form the International Missionary Council (IMC). Its meeting at Jerusalem in 1928 raised sharp questions about the association of missions with colonialism and highlighted the urgency of the church unity issue. Meanwhile parallel movements of "Life and Work" and "Faith and Order" came together to form the World Council of Churches (WCC) in 1948. This provided an institutional instrument through which the goal of visible church unity could be pursued.

NEW THINKING ABOUT MISSION

While the church unity question was rising up the agenda, the concept of mission faced new challenges. As the era of European colonial rule approached its end in many parts of the world, the question arose as to what this would mean for the future of mission. In the minds of many, the missionary movement was inextricably linked with colonialism. The experience of the two World Wars and the Holocaust shattered people's confidence in the validity of a missionary movement apparently based in Europe.

In face of this crisis, the IMC met at Willingen, in Germany, in 1952. It was here that fresh thinking about mission crystallised. Mission was not the product of any particular set of historical circumstances. Its foundations were much deeper and much more permanent. For mission is rooted in the eternal reality of the being and purpose of God. The deepest and defining truth about mission is that it is the mission of God (often invoked in the Latin phrase *missio Dei* = "mission of God").

On this understanding, mission comprises the whole of God's purpose in the world. The church is an instrument—a privileged instrument—of the mission of God. It therefore becomes impossible to separate church and mission. This new understanding of church and mission underpinned the integration of the WCC and IMC in 1961. As a result, the WCC's Commission on World Mission and Evangelism became the institutional heir of Edinburgh 1910.

> The missionary movement of which we are a part has its source in the Triune God Himself. Out of the depths of His love for us, the Father has sent forth His own beloved Son to reconcile all things (*ta panta*) to Himself, that we and all men might, through the Spirit, be made one in Him with the Father in that perfect love which is the very nature of God.[20]

—International Missionary Council, Willingen, 1952

The integration of the IMC and the WCC was not without its critics. There were fears that a focus on evangelism might be lost in the wide agenda of the WCC. Many felt that these fears were justified when the 1960s saw the attention of the WCC apparently absorbed by social and political issues. The 1974 Lausanne Congress on World Evangelization staked its claim to be the true heir of Edinburgh 1910 when it brought the priority of evangelism and personal conversion to centre stage.

Since 1974 "ecumenical" and "evangelical" have become the watchwords of rival camps, each operating a worldwide network. In recent years have come signs that, in a new century, the polarisation is softening as new challenges and new perspectives present themselves. The 2005 Athens conference of the WCC Commission on World Mission and Evangelism included significant representation not only of Evangelicals but also of Roman Catholics, Pentecostals and Independents. Similar breadth of representation is seen in the newly-formed Global Christian Forum and in the General Council of Edinburgh 2010.[21] These initiatives show that, notwithstanding the immense diversity in world Christianity today, there is a widespread consensus that to think mission is to think church unity.

MISSION AND UNITY: TWO SIDES OF ONE COIN

The concern of Edinburgh 1910 for greater unity and cooperation in Christian mission was driven, at first, by strategic and pragmatic goals. Greater cooperation would mean greater effectiveness in the great task of evangelising the world. At the conference, however, deeper concerns emerged about the relation between the unity of the church and the integrity of mission. These concerns have been a major focus of discussion during the 20th century.

God's nature as trinity—Father, Son and Holy Spirit—has been taken as the clue to understanding the unity of the church. The communion of the three persons of the Trinity forms the model and the basis for the unity of the church. Equally, it is the movement within the life of God through which the Father sends the Son to bring salvation to the world which forms the model and the basis for a true understanding of mission. Jesus' life, death and resurrection are therefore the defining reality for Christian mission. This is further underlined by the action of God at Pentecost—the sending of the Holy Spirit, deriving from the Father and sent by the Son to bring his salvation to the world. Both mission and unity have their roots deep in the life of God.

Disciples are sent into the world on the same basis as Jesus was sent by the Father (John 17:18). This is the key to a true understanding of mission. It is not about the aggrandisement of any individual or institution. Rather, it is modelled on the mission of Jesus Christ who "emptied himself" for the sake of others. Vulnerability is the keynote as disciples of Jesus open themselves up to others, seeking to share the love of God which they have found to be transformative. Oppression, domination and subordination are ruled out. Respect for others is the driving force for a mission which combats all that undermines human dignity. Within this ethos, the church seeks to win disciples from among all nations.

As a matter of history, there would be no church had there not first been mission. This points us to the permanent reality that the life of the church arises from the mission of God. There can be no church without mission. The church is "missionary by its very nature". As the church lives out its response to the love of God in Jesus Christ this finds expression in participation in the mission of God. Sacrificial service and faithful witness are integral to the life of the church. "The missionary opening-up of the Church to the world is not an optional activity, but, on the contrary, a fundamental condition for her catholicity."[22]

EVANGELISM—ON A NOTE OF HUMILITY

When Jesus prayed "that they may all be one ... so that the world may believe that you have sent me" (John 17:21), he ensured that the church would never be able to think of unity without thinking of evangelism—and vice versa. After a century of wrestling with this twofold challenge, a consensus emerging today is that the development of common witness is an urgent imperative. Though there may be differences between different streams of Christian tradition which remain unresolved, all can come together to share in evangelism.

By evangelism is meant the dimension of mission which involves a direct and explicit proclamation of the good news of Jesus Christ, with an invitation to conversion, faith and discipleship. Nothing could be more personal. If the challenge and invitation to people as individuals is obscured or blunted then something vital has been lost. At the same time, evangelism is not something private or esoteric. The good news of Jesus Christ is openly addressed to the community, the wider society, the nation, the international community and indeed the entire cosmos.

> Evangelism is the proclamation of the good news accompanied by an invitation to turn away from false absolutes and to turn to the living God, to follow Jesus Christ as one's only Saviour and Lord, to join the community of his Church and to live under the prompting of the Holy Spirit and take the ethics of the kingdom of God as one's guide.[23]

—Jacques Matthey, 2007

There remains today a widespread suspicion of evangelism, since it is thought to operate hand-in-glove with political and economic forces which are seeking to establish domination. Even Edinburgh 1910 was not free of a degree of complicity with the colonialism which prevailed at that time. Its military metaphors of battle and conquest have left a bitter taste, especially in light of the violence experienced by many during the past century. It is therefore imperative to stress that evangelism is not about domination or subjugation. On the contrary, Jesus embraced the role of a servant and "emptied himself". His disciples must do the same if they are truly to commend him to the world today. Unless conducted with genuine humility, evangelism will deservedly lack credibility.

> The proclamation of God's kingdom necessarily demands the prophetic denunciation of all that is incompatible with it. Among the evils we deplore are destructive violence, including institutionalized violence, political corruption, all forms of exploitation of people and of the earth, the undermining of the family, abortion on demand, the drug traffic, and the abuse of human rights. In our concern for the poor, we are distressed by the burden of debt in the two-thirds world. We are also outraged by the inhu-

man conditions in which millions live, who bear God's image as we do. True mission … necessitates entering humbly into other people's worlds, identifying with their social reality, their sorrow and suffering, and their struggles for justice against oppressive powers. This cannot be done without personal sacrifices.[24]

—Lausanne Movement, Manila Manifesto, 1989

One area which requires special sensitivity is competition between churches for members, particularly when one church seeks to recruit members from among the membership of another. Where this is done in ways which contradict the spirit of Christian love, it is rightly condemned as "proselytization". At the same time, no church can "own" its members and sometimes they have good reasons for choosing to move to a new church or denomination. Openness, transparency, mutual respect and, above all, love are required if churches are to support one another and their members in cases where a change of allegiance is being considered.

These tensions are best addressed in the context of commitment to common witness. Where churches are actively committed to working together on the evangelistic task they are much less likely to fall prey to unworthy proselytisation. Energy is then focussed not on inter-church competition but rather on helping one another to engage the new frontiers for mission within the contemporary society.

RECONCILIATION AND HEALING

In a world where many are acutely aware of brokenness and fragmentation, the biblical motifs of reconciliation and healing have come to have strong resonance. This begins among the churches themselves. World Christianity today is a mosaic of great diversity. Sadly, it is not without some bitter divisions and there are many unhealed wounds. It is also a reality that different confessions have different models of unity. The ministry of the

Holy Spirit is needed if diversity is to lead not to opposition and hostility but rather to being complementary, interdependent and harmonious. In this process wounds are healed and we move closer to the unity for which Christ prayed.

On this basis the churches can engage the wider world as healing and reconciling communities. Not claiming any moral high ground but as wounded healer, the church can engage the painful realities of division and conflict between nations and within nations. The healing ministry of Jesus has always informed the practice of mission. It strikes a powerful chord today as, across all the various Christian traditions, a consensus emerges that it is through a ministry of reconciliation and healing that mission best takes effect. For this to have credibility the churches must renew their efforts to resolve their own differences and to foster growing commitment to common witness.

KEY TEXT: JOHN 17:20-26

[Jesus said] "I do not ask for these only, but also for those who will believe in me through their word, that they may all be one, just as you, Father, are in me, and I in you, that they also may be in us, so that the world may believe that you have sent me. The glory that you have given me I have given to them, that they may be one even as we are one. I in them and you in me, that they may become perfectly one, so that the world may know that you sent me and loved them even as you loved me. Father, I desire that they also, whom you have given me, may be with me where I am to see my glory that you have given me because you loved me before the foundation of the world. O righteous Father, even though the world does not know you, I know you, and these know that you have sent me. I made known to them your name, and I will continue to make it known, that the love with which you have loved me may be in them, and I in them."

QUESTIONS FOR DISCUSSION
How do you understand the relationship between mission and unity in the life of the church?

How can we best meet the demands of *both* the imperative of unity *and* the mandate for evangelism?

What needs to be healed in order for the oneness of the church to be more apparent in your context?

PRAYER
Praise be to you, living God, the Father, the Son and the Holy Spirit.
Thank you that unity and diversity lie deep in the life of God.
Forgive us that we turn unity into oppression and diversity into conflict.
Grant that we may cherish one another, valuing each other's history and identity.
Bless your church throughout the world, grant that divisions may be overcome,
and that your church may be united in its great task of taking the gospel to the world.
Help me to play my part in Christ's ministry of reconciliation,
that healing may come to people and to churches and to nations.
For your eternal glory and praise, through Jesus Christ the Lord.
Amen

9

Being the Church in Mission

BEING FOR THE POOR

A stark reality facing us when we consider our world today is the unacceptable levels of poverty which are found everywhere but particularly in the Global South. Some 1,300,000,000 people live in "abject poverty"—defined by the United Nations as living on less than 1US$ per day. The UN's call for decisive action to end the scandal of poverty has been echoed by many governments in the wealthy North. However, the resources committed to achieving this objective are tiny compared with those mobilised to resolve the Northern financial crisis or to acquire destructive weapons.

It is very clear in the Bible that God's priorities are different. When we read the gospels, Jesus' solidarity with the poor, the defenceless and the marginalised shines forth like a beacon. When we follow Jesus we are sure to find ourselves alongside the poor, seeing things with their eyes and working with them for greater empowerment.

In light of this strong biblical emphasis, the church must be constantly mindful of the poor. It stands in active solidarity with those who face homelessness, hunger, diseases, sexual exploitation, HIV/AIDS, profitless labour, drug trafficking, lack of education, disability and untimely death. It must muster its resources to take action to alleviate poverty through provision of food, shelter, healthcare and education. It must, at the same time, be the constant advocate of measures which make for greater justice in the operation of the global economy. Both the compassionate action and the forthright advocacy must be underpinned by constant prayer.

Through experience, the church has learned that poverty, most often, is not an inexplicable misfortune which befalls certain individuals. Nor is it usually the fault of an individual or community that they experience poverty. Of course, there are individual circumstances which can play their part. However, the principal cause of poverty, overwhelmingly, is found in the prevailing power structures which work to the advantage of some and the disadvantage of others. The caste system in India is a classic case. In other contexts the social structures which bestow wealth on some and poverty on others are more subtle but no less real.

A crucial question for the church is whether it mirrors the prevailing power structures or challenges them. The church's mandate, very clearly, is to bring good news to the poor and let the oppressed go free. Yet it is sobering to observe that church life in India often mirrors the caste system which prevails in the wider society. It fails to break with the social hierarchy by developing a community where the same opportunities are open to all. What is made noticeable by the starkness of the caste system can also be found in many contexts in more subtle forms.

> For many within the Dalit community in Bombay (India), their access to resources in the churches has been prevented due to the perpetuation of a hierarchy in the churches that mirrors what is present within the society. As a result, the Christian

ministry has become privatized with the rich having more access to pastoral care because they contribute more economic resources to the church, ultimately producing a fragmented community. So although church numbers have grown, this has coincided with an increase in the number of people begging outside the church premises.[25]

It is a challenging reality that those entrusted with leadership positions in the churches have not always demonstrated the bias to the poor shown by Jesus. In fact, some have sought their own power and wealth in ways which reflect the prevailing patterns of contemporary society. In contrast, the calling of the churches is not only to empathise with the poor but to identify with them through the servant leadership modelled by Jesus. One way the church can do this is by drawing its leadership from among the poor. When poor people cease to be victims and become agents of transformation for their communities, this is a sign that the kingdom of God is coming.

Where it stands in relation to poverty is a barometer of how far the church is being true to its calling in today's world.

MODELLING JUSTICE AND RECONCILIATION

As they look to be a force for justice and reconciliation in today's world, the churches must begin by recognising their own complicity in injustice and alienation in the past. In seeking to resolve ethnic conflict in Kenya, for example, it is important to recognise that much of this revolves around land issues. Scarcity of land is related to the historical fact that large areas were appropriated by Christian missions in the late 19th and early 20th centuries. To be part of the solution, the churches must first acknowledge that they have been part of the problem.

The churches are also challenged to look at their own internal life. Some churches have made deliberate attempts to marginalize other churches. For example, well-established denominations have sometimes been hostile to new movements. Within churches, stratification along class, race, ethnicity, gender, age or abilities is not difficult to find. While the churches have advocated participatory democracy in the political sphere, their witness has often been undermined by evidence of domination and oppression within their own life.

The fault-lines imposed by divisive social issues are there for all to see. Such matters as women in church leadership and the place of gay and lesbian people continue to cause deep division within church life, both locally and globally, both within traditions and between traditions. Since it is unlikely that these issues will be conclusively and universally resolved any time soon, it is imperative that the churches find ways to express their unity in Christ even when there are differing views on important questions.

> Churches have to find a way of acknowledging their brokenness and disagreements, and then seeking the common, "kingdom" ground to enable them to serve together despite the differences.[26]

A special challenge facing our generation is the prevalence of HIV/AIDS. Often the initial response of the churches compounded the problems facing those infected or affected by HIV and AIDS. The virus was viewed as being associated with immorality; silence and denial prevailed in the churches, and stigma was applied to those found to be HIV positive. Having been part of the problem, in many cases churches are now emerging as part of the solution. They have been distinguished by their capacity to inform, educate, motivate and support behaviour change within communities, and their ability to advocate at national, regional and international forums on behalf of those people affected by HIV/AIDS.

CHURCH IN THE CITY

In a world where more and more people are living in cities, the question of how to be the church in the city is a critical one. Historic patterns of ministry often do not connect well with the social landscape emerging in the great cities of today. It is time to evolve new forms of fellowship and witness which are closely in tune with the life of the city.

It is important to recognise the dynamic nature of the city and to connect with people where they are. There are different flows of people within the social space of the city and each needs to be met in an appropriate way. The variety of ministries offered by the Edinburgh City Mission gives a sample of what can be done:

- A drop-in centre with a cafe provides a peaceful place to chat and relax in a part of the city where alcohol and drug abuse makes everyday life hazardous.
- A "Basics Bank" supplies food and toiletries for an eight-week period to people who have fallen on hard times and lack life's essentials. Staff meet with clients to offer practical guidance as well as sharing the gospel of Christ when appropriate. In the entertainment area of the city there is a centre which opens late on Friday and Saturday nights, offering a ministry to clubbers.
- Outside the University Library a stall offers hot drinks and the opportunity for students to discuss the good news of Jesus Christ.
- A care van offers support to homeless people, providing food, clothing and blankets, as well as a listening ear.

It is a wide-ranging ministry, meeting people at the point of their need and losing no opportunity to share the good news of Jesus Christ.

As churches engage with the city and seek to meet its challenges they find that others are working on issues of shared concern. There is often a place for the churches at the civic table and they are valued partners in meeting the challenge of urban regeneration. As they make common cause with others it is important that churches safeguard the integrity of their own faith and values. At times, the church initiatives which have led to a high level of involvement in civic engagement and social action have drifted away from the evangelistic purpose of faith-sharing and discipleship. These two dimensions of Christian witness need to be constantly held in tension, rather than allowing one to flourish at the expense of the other.

Churches often have significant property in the cities, particularly where they are long established as in Europe. As population patterns change, sometimes quite rapidly, there is need to think creatively about buildings. It may be, for example, that an historic denomination no longer needs a large city-centre church but there is great potential for it to be used as a community resource or handed on to an immigrant church which is growing in the area. To make the most of inherited property resources involves discernment, the ability to think strategically and a willingness to look beyond the narrow interests of one particular group or denomination.

CHURCH ON THE MOVE

Mobility is a major feature of contemporary society. Gone are the days, in many parts of the world, where families remain in the same place generation upon generation. Today's economy requires people to be mobile and the church has to adapt to this new pattern of life. Indeed, the new pattern presents a great opportunity for mission since when people move they can take the gospel with them, or perhaps they may encounter the gospel for the first time.

Movements of Christian mission today often find expression through a particular diaspora. For example, from South Korea, Ghana and Nigeria have emerged extensive diaspora movements which have established churches and pioneered fresh Christian witness in many places. Pastoral care for their own community is often combined with a strong sense of mission to their new place. In the UK, for example, it is Black Majority Churches which have pioneered "Street Pastors". This is an initiative which places suitably trained Christians on the streets to engage with young people in locations where they congregate at night and often come under the influence of drugs or alcohol. In urban areas it is common for a number of churches to come together and share together in organising this outreach.

> The Filipino experience in diaspora missions also illustrates the providential grace of God in spite of the painful past of colonization of the Philippines by Western powers and sorrowful financial state of contemporary Filipino society. Hence, the sovereignty of God is evidently shown in the scattering of Filipinos globally for a purpose. It is diaspora mission in action—those being scattered have become gatherers for the Kingdom in many nations.[27]

A significant challenge is often presented when the new immigrant church encounters the long-established local church. Though they serve the same Lord, their experience of life and their styles of worship can often be so different that it is difficult to strike up a positive relationship. Mobility and migration have created the possibility for local churches to demonstrate the worldwide character of Christian faith. On the ground, however, it appears that people often prefer to worship with those who share their background and ethnicity. Are we missing an opportunity to experience and to demonstrate the catholicity of the church? Are our attitudes completely free from the influence of racism? Do we allow our unity in Christ to be compromised by economic, cultural or linguistic differences?

When immigration is a major influence on the life of the church, there is need for sound understanding of the intergenerational dynamics that emerge. It is common for "age wars" to break out when generational perspectives clash. The first generation of immigrants tends to be concerned about maintaining their identity. The second generation are more open in terms of engaging with the host society. Traditional gender roles often change in the new circumstances, both in terms of breadwinning and religious functions. For all concerned it is a challenging transition.

Mission today is "from everywhere to everywhere". For some it is a new thought that they are now on the receiving end of mission. For others it is amazing to think that they are the missionaries of today. For all, there is the opportunity to hear the gospel in new ways, come to a greater appreciation of its range and depth, and to open up new paths to reach others with its message.

Key Text: Luke 4:16-21

And Jesus came to Nazareth, where he had been brought up. And as was his custom, he went to the synagogue on the Sabbath day, and he stood up to read. And the scroll of the prophet Isaiah was given to him. He unrolled the scroll and found the place where it was written, "The Spirit of the Lord is upon me, because he has anointed me to proclaim good news to the poor. He has sent me to proclaim liberty to the captives and recovery of sight to the blind, to set at liberty those who are oppressed, to proclaim the year of the Lord's favour." And he rolled up the scroll and gave it back to the attendant and sat down. And the eyes of all in the synagogue were fixed on him. And he began to say to them, "Today this scripture has been fulfilled in your hearing."

QUESTIONS FOR DISCUSSION

What does it mean today, locally and globally, to be good news to the poor?

In what ways does your church succeed, and in what ways does it fail, to be a model of justice and reconciliation in your context?

What at the implications for the life of the church of increasing mobility and migration worldwide?

PRAYER

I worship you, O God, because of your great love for all,
and especially for the despised, the outcast, the poor and the rejected.
Grant me, I pray, the wisdom and the courage to see things your way,
and to let the outcome for the poor determine my priorities and my
actions.
I praise you that you are the God of the new departure, the Lord of
the journey.
Be present with all who travel today to begin their life in a new place.
Grant that your church may be light on its feet,
adapting to new dynamics and meeting people where they are with
your good news.
All for your glory, through Jesus Christ, the beginning and the end.
Amen

Resources

Websites
Edinburgh 2010: www.edinburgh2010.org

Global Christian Forum: www.globalchristianforum.org

Lausanne Movement: www.lausanne.org

Pontifical Council for Promoting Christian Unity: www.
    vatican.va/roman_curia/pontifical_councils

World Council of Churches: www.oikumene.org

World Evangelical Alliance: www.worldevangelicals.org

Books
Balia, Daryl & Kirsteen Kim ed., *Edinburgh 2010: Witnessing to Christ Today*, Oxford: Regnum, 2010.

Douglas, J.D. ed., *Proclaim Christ Until He Comes: Calling the Whole Church to Take the Whole Gospel to the Whole World*, Minneapolis: World Wide Publications, 1990.

Johnson, Todd M. & Kenneth R. Ross ed., *Atlas of Global*

Christianity 1910-2010, Edinburgh: Edinburgh University Press, 2009.

Kerr, David A. & Kenneth R. Ross ed., *Edinburgh 2010: Mission Then and Now*, Oxford: Regnum, 2009.

Kim, Kirsteen, *Joining in with the Spirit: Connecting World Church and Local Mission*, London: Epworth, 2010.

Matthey, Jacques ed., *"You are the light of the World": Statements on Mission by the World Council of Churches 1980-2005*, Geneva: World Council of Churches, 2005.

Robert, Dana L., *Christian Mission: How Christianity Became a World Religion*, Oxford: Wiley-Blackwell, 2009.

Ross, Kenneth R., *Edinburgh 2010: Springboard for Mission*, Pasadena: William Carey International University Press, 2009.

Sanneh, Lamin, *Disciples of All Nations: Pillars of World Christianity*, New York: Oxford University Press, 2008.

Stanley, Brian, *The World Missionary Conference, Edinburgh 1910*, Grand Rapids & Cambridge: Eerdmans, 2009.

Walls, Andrew & Cathy Ross ed., *Mission in the 21st Century: Exploring the Five Marks of Global Mission*, London: Darton, Longman & Todd, 2008.

Endnotes

1. Kenneth R. Ross, *Edinburgh 2010: Springboard for Mission*, Pasadena: William Carey International University Press, 2009.

2. Samuel Escobar, quoted in Daryl Balia & Kirsteen Kim ed, *Edinburgh 2010: Witnessing to Christ Today*, Oxford: Regnum, 2010, chapter 5.

3. Quoted in Balia & Kim, *Edinburgh 2010*, chapter 1.

4. Serah Wambua, "Mission Spirituality and Authentic Discipleship: An African Reflection"; quoted in Balia & Kim, *Edinburgh 2010*, chapter 9.

5. Valentin Kozhuharov, "Mission in an Orthodox Christian Context"; quoted in Balia & Kim, *Edinburgh 2010*, chapter 9.

6. René Padilla, quoted in Balia & Kim, *Edinburgh 2010*, chapter 9.

7. Stan Mackay, quoted in Balia & Kim, *Edinburgh 2010*, chapter 4.

8. Archbishop of St Boniface, quoted in Balia & Kim, *Edinburgh 2010*, chapter 4.

9. Quoted in Balia & Kim, *Edinburgh 2010*, chapter 4.

10. Ian Morrison, quoted in Balia & Kim, *Edinburgh 2010*, chapter 4.

11. Apology to the Aboriginal peoples of Canada by United Church of Canada Moderator Robert Smith, 1986; quoted in Balia & Kim, *Edinburgh 2010*, chapter 4.

12. Wendy Fletcher, quoted in Balia & Kim, *Edinburgh 2010*, chapter 4.

13. *Ibid.*

14. Quoted in Balia & Kim, *Edinburgh 2010*, chapter 3.

15. Education in Relation to the Christianisation of National Life, Report of Commission III, World Missionary Conference, Edinburgh & London: Oliphant, Anderson and Ferrier, 1910, pp. 371-72; quoted in Balia & Kim, *Edinburgh 2010*, chapter 6.

16. Balia & Kim, *Edinburgh 2010*, chapter 6.

17. *Ibid.*

18. "The Way of Dialogue", Appendix 6 of the Lambeth Conference 1998; quoted in Balia & Kim, *Edinburgh 2010*, chapter 6.

19. World Missionary Conference, 1910, *Report of Commission VIII: Co-operation and the Promotion of Unity.* Edinburgh & London: Oliphant, Anderson & Ferrier, 1910, p. 5; quoted in Balia & Kim, *Edinburgh 2010*, chapter 8.

20. Norman Goodall ed., *Missions under the Cross. Addresses Delivered at the Enlarged Meeting of the International Missionary Council at Willingen, Germany, 1952; with Statements Issued by the Meeting,* London: Edinburgh House Press, 1953, p. 189; quoted in Balia & Kim, *Edinburgh 2010*, chapter 8.

21. See www.globalchristianforum.org; www.edinburgh2010.org

22. Athanasios N. Papathanasiou, 'Is Mission a Consequence of the Catholicity of the Church? An Orthodox Perspective', *International Review of Mission,* Vol. 90/359 (October 2001), pp. 409-16; quoted in Balia & Kim, *Edinburgh 2010*, chapter 8.

23. Jacques Matthey, "Evangelism, Still the Enduring Test of Our Ecumenical and Missionary Calling", *International Review of Mission*, Vol. 96/382-83 (2007), p. 355; quoted in Balia & Kim, *Edinburgh 2010*, chapter 8.

24. Lausanne Movement, Manila Manifesto, www.lausanne.org (accessed 18 January 2010).

25. Balia & Kim, *Edinburgh 2010*, chapter 7.

26. *Ibid.*

27. Sadiri Joy Tira & Enoch Wan, "The Filipino Experience in Diaspora Missions: A Case Study of Christian Communities in Contemporary Contexts"; quoted in Balia & Kim, *Edinburgh 2010*, chapter 7.

94559328R00061

Made in the USA
Lexington, KY
31 July 2018